THE PRACTICAL STEP-BY-STEP GUIDE TO
SCRAPBOOKING

sk8

THE PRACTICAL STEP-BY-STEP GUIDE TO
SCRAPBOOKING

HOW TO DISPLAY YOUR TREASURED PHOTOGRAPHS AND MEMORIES WITH FUN AND FABULOUS SCRAPBOOK PAGES

A WEALTH OF INSPIRING IDEAS WITH MORE THAN 65 STEP-BY-STEP PROJECTS AND OVER 400 PHOTOGRAPHS

ALISON LINDSAY

southwater

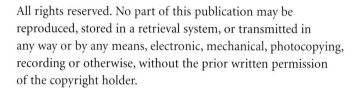

DEDICATION
For Alex

This edition is published by Southwater,
an imprint of Anness Publishing Ltd
Hermes House, 88–89 Blackfriars Road
London SE1 8HA
tel. 020 7401 2077; fax 020 7633 9499

www.southwaterbooks.com; www.annesspublishing.com

If you like the images in this book and would like to investigate
using them for publishing, promotions or advertising, please visit
our website www.practicalpictures.com for more information.

UK agent: The Manning Partnership Ltd
tel. 01225 478444; fax 01225 478440
sales@manning-partnership.co.uk

UK distributor: Book Trade Services; tel. 0116 2759086;
fax 0116 2759090; uksales@booktradeservices.com;
exportsales@booktradeservices.com

North American agent/distributor: National Book Network
tel. 301 459 3366; fax 301 429 5746
www.nbnbooks.com

Australian agent/distributor: Pan Macmillan Australia
tel. 1300 135 113; fax 1300 135 103
customer.service@macmillan.com.au

New Zealand agent/distributor: David Bateman Ltd
tel. (09) 415 7664; fax (09) 415 8892

Publisher: Joanna Lorenz
Editorial Director: Helen Sudell
Editors: Ann Kay and Simona Hill
Designer: Terry Jeavons
Photographers: Mark Wood and Paul Bricknell
Editorial Reader: Emily Adenipekun
Production Controller: Steve Lang

A CIP catalogue record for this book is available from the
British Library.

Previously published as part of a larger volume, *The Complete
Practical Guide to Scrapbooking*

ETHICAL TRADING POLICY
Because of our ongoing ecological investment programme,
you, as our customer, can have the pleasure and reassurance
of knowing that a tree is being cultivated on your behalf to
naturally replace the materials used to make the book you are
holding. For further information about this scheme, go to
www.annesspublishing.com/trees

PUBLISHER'S NOTE
Although the advice and information in this book are believed to be
accurate and true at the time of going to press, neither the author
nor the publisher can accept any legal responsibility or liability for
any errors or omissions that may be made.

ACKNOWLEDGEMENTS
Alison Lindsay p10, p11, p12, p13, p14, p15, p16, p17, p18, p19,
p21, p22, p23, p24tr and b, p25, p29tr, p30 tint box, p31, p32, p33,
p34, p35, p37, p39, p40, p41, p42, p43, p44, p45, p46, p47.
Penny Boylan p20t, p24tl, p28b, p29, p30l and c, p36, p38, p42cr.
Joy Aitman p20b, p52tr, p55br. Cheryl Owen p48, p49, p50, p51,
p52, p53, p54, p55, p56, p57. Elaine Hewson p62–73 and all other
digital scrapbook pages.
Thanks also to May Taylor, Claire Longdon, Cher King,
Pauline Craik and Sue Davies.
Thanks to the following suppliers: Hot Off the Press, Inc., Paper
Cellar Ltd, Glue Dots, Efco Hobby Products, Arty's, Fibermark,
Grassroots, Magic Mesh, F. W. Bramell & Co Ltd, Creative Memories,
Junkitz, and Clearsnap Inc.

CONTENTS

INTRODUCTION

A century ago having a photograph taken was a notable event, which required a trip to a photographer's studio, often with family and friends, each dressed in their Sunday best. For later generations, having access to portable camera equipment meant photographs could be taken more easily and by amateurs, but still at a relatively high cost. Today's innovative digital cameras and computer technology means that we can all take photographs and plenty of them, and store them on our computers, or learn to process them ourselves using equipment that is easy to use and to buy. To make full use of our photographs and display them to best effect, the age-old craft of scrapbooking has made a revival. In fact, a whole industry has evolved, with craft manufacturers selling tailor-made designs and products to inspire us with new ideas and ways to be creative.

Today's scrapbooks are made up of highly designed, colour-co-ordinated themed pages, each displaying our treasured memories to best effect and turning them into fabulous visual records for posterity. Scrapbooks contain photographs, but they are not just photograph albums. Backgrounds for images can be put together using readily

▲ *Old black-and-white photographs show how times change when compared to today's colour prints.*

available scrapbook papers, many designed with specific themes in mind, or you could even create your own using the ideas included here. Each photograph can be cut to size, with fancy scissors to make a decorative edging, and then carefully positioned on the background in much the same way that you would decide how to hang pictures on a wall. Make frames for each of them, if you like, and then add diary details explaining the event, the date, the people involved, the mood of the occasion and the special memories you have of the time – all in a script chosen by you.

To the basic page you can add all kinds of different mementoes – a treasured handmade card for a first birthday party page, for example, confetti collected from a wedding breakfast table for a contemporary wedding page, theatre tickets from a day out with friends for a friendship page, a small painting by a first grandchild, for a family page – whatever is appropriate to the event and the people involved. The intention is to produce pages for your album that have a cohesive look, each telling their own story, and helping to preserve special memories.

▼ *Flowers make a colourful addition to a scrapbook page, as well as a good way of recording the successes of the past gardening year.*

This beautiful book contains everything you need to know to be able to create your own scrapbook pages from scratch. All you need to do to start is to make a selection of your favourite photographs and organize them in a meaningful way. For example, you might like to create album pages of the children in your extended family, or pages containing old sepia prints that display your family tree. For a keen gardener, you could put together pages that show the progress of a burgeoning garden design, or a much-loved landscape in different seasons.

Information is provided to help you take the best photographs possible, considering the subject matter and its background carefully. There are then hints and tips to help you choose appropriate colours and patterns that will enhance your photographs. There are plenty of ideas for background treatments, such as using textured papers and layering cut or torn papers over the top to create a collage, or using paint effects to add colour to plain backgrounds. There are ideas for stamping patterns on to a background, creating antiquing effects, even stencilling designs around your chosen images.

Once the background is established the fun begins, embellishing the album pages. Whatever your artistic ability or inclination, plenty of ideas are presented here to help you make the most interesting and creative

▼ *Teabag folding (printed papers the size of teabags) is a papercraft that can be used to enhance a favourite photograph.*

▲ *Photographs of a family trip to the seaside are complemented with soft muted colours and wave-like papers.*

pages possible. Embellish gift tags with paints and stamps, wrap them with ribbons, and attach them to the page with decorative brads or colourful staples. Fold teabag papers into flower shapes or create a paper patchwork. Then add texture using appropriate mementoes, or create your own decorations using beads, embroidery, modelled clay shapes, embossed metal foil or creative wirework. If you enjoy dabbling on a computer, information is provided to help you make digital album pages, each containing all the elements of a hand-assembled page. The finishing touch is to add descriptive text, which can be hand-written or computer-generated. Instructions are provided for both.

The final chapter of the book presents more than 60 beautiful scrapbook designs for album pages, covers and memory boxes. There are plenty of styles of work to help inspire your own scrapbooks, from those with a plain and simple graphic quality to highly decorative and artistically produced designs. There are examples of a range of the most popular topics for scrapbooks – weddings, children, animals, family and friends and heritage. Whatever your preference, there are techniques and tips here that will teach you a new decorative treatment to add colour and character to your scrapbook pages.

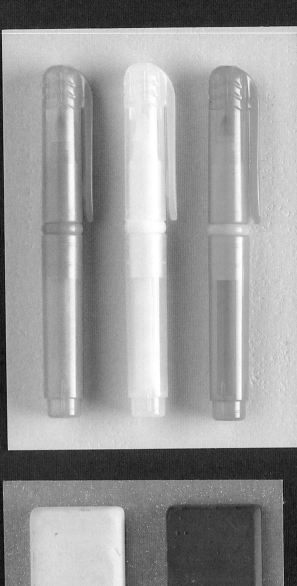

Getting started

Creating album pages is about encapsulating life's precious moments in a way that feels right for you. As you gain experience you'll have plenty of ideas for presentation and develop your own personal style. There are lots of ways to make exciting scrapbooks, and there are tips to guide you through your ideas to help you make the most of your irreplaceable prints and memorabilia.

Craft stores are bursting with seductive pieces of kit and decorative materials, and it's very easy to get carried away buying stickers, die stamps and fancy cutters that appeal to your sense of colour and style before you have any clear idea of what you'll do with them. This section offers a guide to the materials and equipment available, to help you match the possibilities to the items you want to display. Step-by-step instructions will take you through all the different photographic and craft techniques you need to make beautiful, meaningful pages.

EQUIPMENT AND MATERIALS

It's easy to get carried away by the vast range of fancy punches, stamps and stickers available for scrapbooking. Start with the basics – album pages, scissors and adhesive – and add to your collection gradually as you develop your themes.

Cutting tools

Whatever the style of your albums, impeccably accurate cutting is essential for good-looking results. Bad trimming can ruin your precious pictures, so invest in good scissors and knives.

▶ *Cutting decorative edges.*

Template sheets

Shaped plastic templates

Wavy-edged trimmer

Corner cutter

Miniature knives

Metal ruler and craft knife

These give total control over where and how you cut. The knife blade should always be retracted or covered when not in use. If safety is a concern, a guillotine or trimmer may be a better option.

▼ *Cutting straight lines.*

Small scissors

Scissors

Decorative-edged scissors

Cutting mat

Straight trimmer or guillotine

Use this to trim paper or photographs with straight edges. All trimmers have a grid printed or embossed on to the cutting surface, to help you measure accurately. Some have interchangeable blades that cut patterned lines as well as straight ones.

Metal rule

Craft knife

Straight trimmer

Plastic templates

▶ *Cutting small decorative shapes.*

Punches

Speciality cutters

There are all kinds of cutters available that make it easy to cut photographs and mats into decorative shapes. Placing a template over a photograph allows you to see what size to cut. Templates and cutters are suitable for use together.

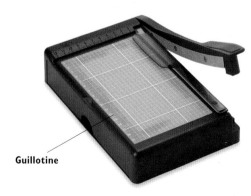

Guillotine

Templates

A wide range of lightweight templates provide different cropping options, and are easy to store. Use a pencil with the template to trace a shape on to a photograph or paper, then cut along the drawn line with scissors.

Punches

Simple small shapes look striking when punched from coloured card. Larger shapes can also be used to cut out the important part of a photograph. Shaped punches are available in hundreds of designs, and can be combined for added impact: for example, several hearts can be assembled together to create the petals of a flower.

Scissors

It is useful to have two pairs of scissors: a large pair for cutting straight lines and a small pair for trimming around decorative shapes and templates. Blades with pointed tips make it easier to cut out intricate shapes.

Decorative-edged scissors

Used sparingly, these add a fancy touch to mats and trims, although it is not advisable to use them on photographs. They work best when cutting a straight edge or a gentle curve.

Adhesives

Many different kinds of adhesive will work well on paper and card (card stock). Make sure any you use are labelled acid-free so that your photographs will not deteriorate when in contact with them.

Glue sticks

These are a cheap and easy way to stick light items such as punched shapes, but some glue sticks are not strong enough to hold photographs in position permanently. Although the glue takes some time to dry, it does not need to be left flat while drying.

Spray adhesive

Both permanent and repositionable adhesives are available in spray form – the latter allows for something that is stuck down to be peeled off and then reapplied. Spray outside or in a well-ventilated room, so that the fumes can disperse. To prevent the spray going everywhere, it is a good idea to place items in a large box, and direct the spray into that. No drying time is required.

Foam pads

These can be used to raise an element on a layout, making it appear three-dimensional. For greater height, you can stick two or more pads together before mounting your item. Use scissors to trim the pads if they are too large, but clean the scissor blades afterwards.

Glue dots and glue lines

These are available in different sizes and thicknesses, and with permanent or repositionable adhesive. The glue is tacky and will hold most items securely. No drying time is required.

Double-sided tape

Whether as a single sheet, pre-cut into squares, or on a continuous roll, this is a clean, easy way to glue most items. Long strips can be used to create borders by applying a piece of tape, removing the backing, then pouring beads or glitter over the exposed tape. Use the same technique with small shapes punched from a sheet. No drying time is required.

Tape dispensers

These allow for the convenient application of a square or line of adhesive, making it easy to glue the edge of unusual or angled shapes. Refills are available for most designs, making them economical too. No drying time is required.

PVA (white) glue

This will hold most items in place, including awkward or three-dimensional items such as shells or charms. The work must be left flat while the glue dries. To cover an album or box, brush glue diluted with water over a sheet of paper and wrap it around the sides.

Photo corners

If you prefer to avoid glueing your photographs permanently, mount them with photo corners. Because the adhesive is on the corner and not the photograph, the picture can be removed later if necessary. Clear photo corners are the most useful, but coloured ones are also available. Gold, silver or black ones look good on heritage or wedding layouts. No drying time is required.

Masking tape

This is useful for temporarily attaching stencils to a layout, or for lifting stickers from their backing sheet.

Sticker sheets

Sticker borders

▲ *Stickers.*

Glue for vellum

Specially made "invisible" glue dots are needed when working with vellum, to avoid the adhesive showing through the sheet. Alternatively, vellum can be attached using spray adhesive.

Stickers

As well as being a decorative element, stickers can be positioned to attach vellum, photographs or journaling blocks to a layout. Choose large scale stickers if you want to stick a heavy item down.

▼ *Adhesive materials*

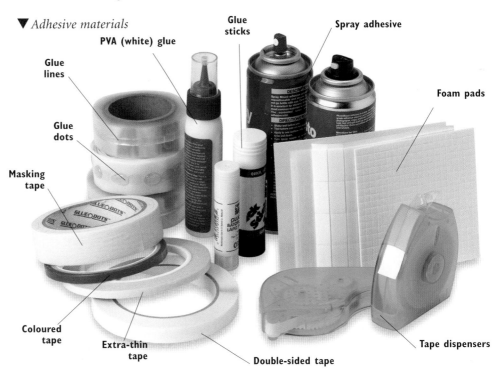

Glue sticks

PVA (white) glue

Spray adhesive

Glue lines

Glue dots

Foam pads

Masking tape

Coloured tape

Extra-thin tape

Double-sided tape

Tape dispensers

Paper and card

Good paper makes a world of difference to your designs, so always buy the best quality you can afford, and make sure it is acid-free to keep your photographs in perfect condition.

Page kits

Sometimes helpful for beginners, page kits combine paper with matching stickers or other embellishments and offer an easy way to create co-ordinated layouts quickly. They are designed to suit a range of themes and cover many different subjects.

Self-coloured card (stock)

This is the basis for many scrapbook pages, and its firmness provides an ideal surface to support photographs and embellishments. Card may be smooth or textured to resemble natural surfaces such as linen. It is available from art and craft suppliers, as single sheets or in multi-packs. Save scraps for paper piecing and matting photos.

Patterned paper

There are thousands of patterned papers available to match almost any theme, event or mood. Papers may be purchased individually, in books or multi-packs; the latter offer better value, but not all the sheets may be to your taste. A folder of patterned paper scraps is useful since many layouts can be attractively embellished using small scraps of paper.

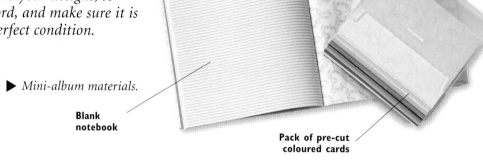

▶ *Mini-album materials.*

Blank notebook

Pack of pre-cut coloured cards

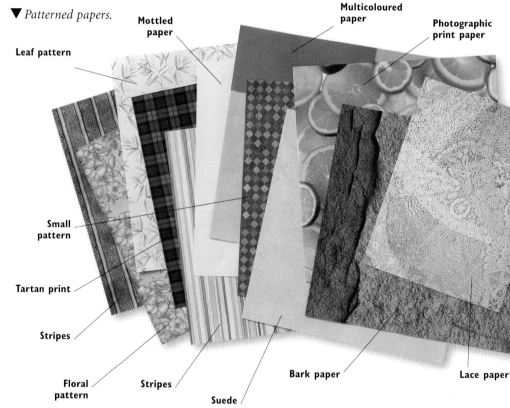

▼ *Patterned papers.*

Leaf pattern

Mottled paper

Multicoloured paper

Photographic print paper

Small pattern

Tartan print

Stripes

Floral pattern

Stripes

Suede paper

Bark paper

Lace paper

▼ *Self-coloured card.*

Glitter card

Textured and embossed paper

These tactile papers give a design texture and depth without adding bulk. Some papers resemble leather or fabric, while others have stitching or metallic embossing to add richness.

Mulberry paper

The fibres used to create this paper are light but very strong. Do not use scissors to cut the paper; instead, "draw" a damp paintbrush across the paper, then tear apart, leaving soft, feathery edges.

Photographic print paper

Some patterned papers offer photographic or naturalistic representations of everyday objects. These can overwhelm a layout if they compete with your own photographs, so restrict them to accents.

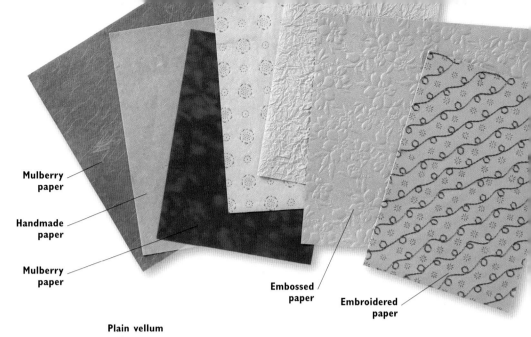

▶ *Textured and embossed papers.*

Mulberry paper

Handmade paper

Mulberry paper

Embossed paper

Embroidered paper

Suede paper
This mimics the texture and appearance of real suede, and so is perfect for representing that material.

Glitter and pearlescent paper
The soft sheen of pearlescent paper is ideal for baby or wedding layouts, while brighter glitter sheets can be used as colourful accents for party pages.

Cut and mini-album packs
Pre-cut small paper packs are available for matting or mini-albums.

Lace papers
These delicate papers mimic the soft colours and patterns of lace without adding weight to the pages, and are perfect for wedding or heritage layouts.

Vellum
Being translucent, vellum gives a soft look to paper or photographs placed underneath it. Patterned vellum can be layered over plain or patterned paper to create a romantic look, and mini-envelopes made from vellum half-conceal the souvenirs they hold. If a photograph you want to use is a little out of focus, you can disguise this by slipping it behind vellum.

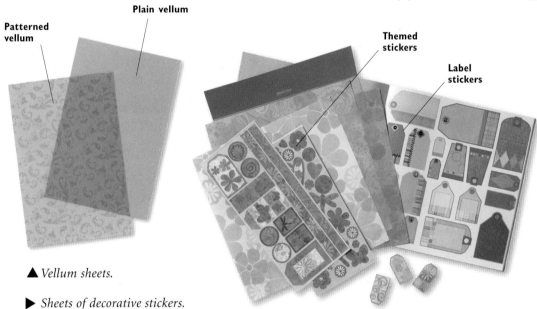

Patterned vellum

Plain vellum

Themed stickers

Label stickers

▲ *Vellum sheets.*

▶ *Sheets of decorative stickers.*

ALBUM BINDINGS

Your album can be of any size, but you will probably find that a 30cm/12in square format offers the best scope for creating satisfying layouts. Loose-leaf albums give the most flexibility, and there are basically three methods of binding pages into them.

Ring binder albums
These are the cheapest way to display layouts, which can be slipped into clear plastic page protectors. Extra page protectors can be added to expand the album. As the ring binding lies between the two pages and distracts the eye, ring binders are best used to present single-page layouts.

Post-bound albums
These albums conceal the posts binding the page protectors together, so a double layout can be viewed without distracting elements. They are available in a wide range of sizes and designs. Extra page protectors may be inserted by unscrewing the posts and adding extenders.

Strap-hinge albums
Plastic hinges slide through loops on the spines of these album pages to create an infinitely extendable album. Each page is an integral part of this kind of album, so background paper needs to be glued on top (known as "wallpapering") to change the layout base.

Notebooks
Any kind of notebook may be used as a scrapbook, especially if a smaller gift album is being created. Decorate plain notebooks by painting or covering with paper, and add embellishments for a unique look. Don't forget to leave room for a title page before the first layout.

Embellishments

This is where the fun really starts, but it's important to keep the focus of attention on your own photographs and memorabilia: make sure the decorative elements enhance the theme of your page rather than dominate it.

▶ *Stickers and adhesive borders.*

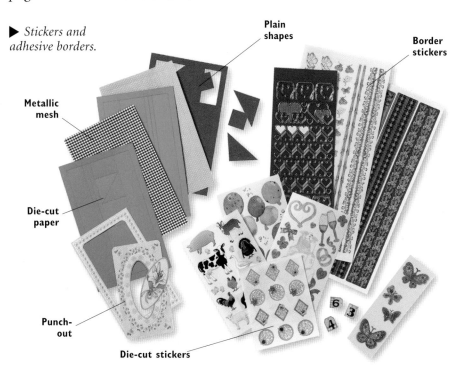

▶ *Photo mounts and templates.*

▲ *Fabric pockets and attachments add interest to a layout.*

Stickers

A staple of scrapbooking, stickers are available in every conceivable colour, size and design, and make it easy to embellish a page quickly. Popular characters are represented on stickers, as well as traditional themes such as Christmas and weddings. If you want to make a sticker more substantial, apply it to white card and cut round it, then mount the shape on a foam pad.

Fabric stickers

These are printed on fabric to add textural interest to a layout. For a homespun look, fray some of the threads at the edges of the sticker.

3D stickers

These are built up from two or more layers of card, ready to be added to a page. Popular themes include babies and travel, and many are also suitable for making greetings cards.

Punch-outs

Shapes die-cut from sheets of card are known as punch-outs, as they need to be pressed out of the backing sheet. They are usually simple shapes, and may be coloured. Printed shapes, or those carrying titles, embellish a layout quickly, and can create a consistent style throughout an album.

Stamping

Use stamps to create a theme on background paper. Stamped images can be coloured, cut out and used like stickers to lend an accent colour or design to a layout. Choose inks in colours that complement the layout, or scribble a felt-tip pen over a stamp, spray lightly with water, then press down. Alphabet stamps are useful for titles.

▼ *Collect postcards, currency and timetables as travel mementoes.*

Paint

Acrylic paint can be used to create any design on backing paper, and the huge range of colours available means you can match any shade in a photograph. Ready-mixed paint in tubes is easy to apply and very fine lines can be drawn using a nib.

Templates

All kinds of templates are available to help you customize layouts. They are an economical option since it is easy to create many different looks with just one template.

Fibres

Lengths of fibre add softness and texture to layouts, and provide contrast with the flatness and hard edges of card and paper. Luxurious knitting wool or ribbons can also be used. Mixed packs can be bought already colour co-ordinated. Try wrapping fibres round the bottom of a photograph, or threading a handful through a tag.

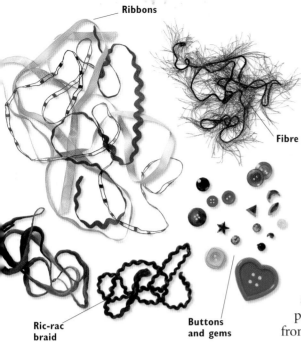

Ribbons

Fibre

Ric-rac braid

Buttons and gems

▲ *Fibres, braids and buttons can be used as borders for pictures or to hold items in place.*

Buttons and gems

Stitch or stick these to a layout as embellishments, or to anchor journaling blocks. You could use a gem to dot the "i" in a title, or scatter several in the corner of a photograph. Delicate pearl buttons are especially suited to baby themes or heritage layouts.

Memorabilia

Real or replica memorabilia adds significance to a layout. When you go travelling, for example, save ephemera such as tickets, timetables and restaurant bills to combine with your photographs. Failing the real thing, you can buy a replica pack. Foreign stamps, used or unused, and paper currency are other authentic additions.

Memorabilia pockets

Tuck small items of memorabilia in pockets to keep them safe but accessible. Pockets that have clear fronts allow you to see what's inside without taking it out.

Attachments

There are lots of specialist attachments available now, which can be kept as they are or further embellished by sanding, painting or stitching. Tuck a special souvenir in a pre-made pocket, or hang a key or zipper pull from a length of ribbon.

Metal

Embellishments sold for scrapbooks have been specially coated to prevent damage to layouts. Use brads or eyelets to fix vellum or tags in place. Thread ribbon or fibres through charms, or place a tiny key next to a heart. Photo turns are attached with brads and can hold hidden journaling closed but accessible. For quick attachment of ribbons, use coloured staples.

Adhesive mesh

This is available in strips or sheets and quickly adds texture to a layout. Dab ink or chalk over the surface then peel off, to give a shadowed texture pattern on paper.

Slide mounts

Cover these in paper or paint, then use as tiny picture frames or to highlight part of a photograph.

Paper charms

Embossed printed and foiled charms can be cut out and added to layouts.

▼ *Paper charms.*

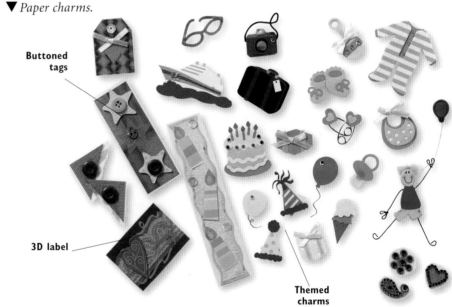

Buttoned tags

3D label

Themed charms

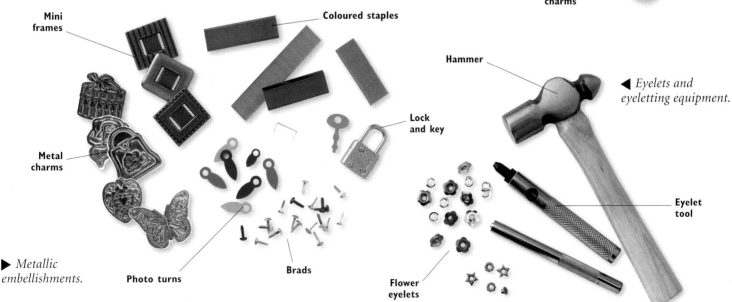

Mini frames

Coloured staples

Metal charms

Photo turns

Brads

Flower eyelets

Lock and key

Hammer

◄ *Eyelets and eyeletting equipment.*

Eyelet tool

▶ *Metallic embellishments.*

Lettering

The words you add to your layouts add an all-important dimension. Use the title to establish the theme of the page, bringing out the character of the layout in your treatment of the main word or perhaps an illuminated initial.

Letter templates

Use these in reverse to trace individual letters on to the back of your chosen paper, then flip over, to avoid having to erase pencil lines. Or use right side up to trace a title directly on to a layout, then colour with pencils or pens.

Letter stickers

The quickest and easiest way to add titles to your pages is with adhesive stickers. Align the bases of the letters along a ruler or use a special plastic guide for curved lines of lettering. Mix colours and styles for a fun approach. Letter squares can be used in both positive and negative forms, making them versatile and economical. Tweezers or a crocodile clip are useful in helping to place letter stickers accurately.

Cut-out letters

These are available in sheets or as part of themed paper collections, and make good decorative initials. Cut them out individually and glue down, or mount on foam pads for added dimension. A large number of styles are available to suit any scrapbook theme.

Buttons

Some manufacturers offer sets of letters in a range of different formats, such as small buttons. You could glue or stitch them on to a layout, or thread a name on thin ribbon and drape it over a photograph. Use a single button for the initial letter of a word to highlight it.

▼ *Lettering stickers and tools.*

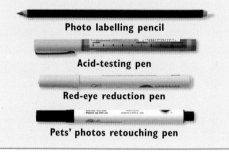

Photo labelling pencil

Acid-testing pen

Red-eye reduction pen

Pets' photos retouching pen

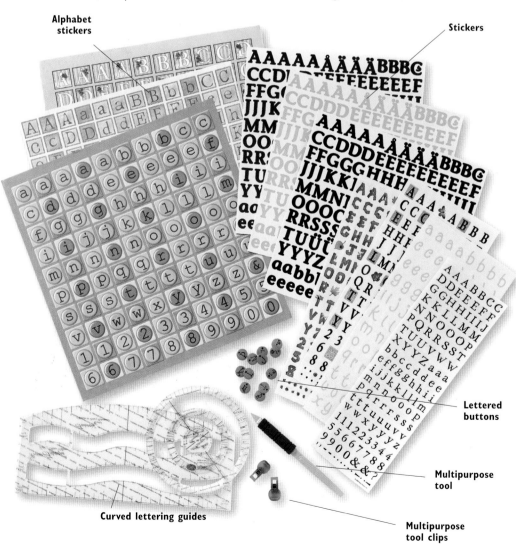

Alphabet stickers

Stickers

Lettered buttons

Multipurpose tool

Curved lettering guides

Multipurpose tool clips

▲ *Use lettering templates to trace individual letters for titles, then fill in with ink or pens or cut out and glue in place on the page.*

Tools for journaling

While titles and captions can identify the people in the pictures, journaling goes further, explaining the background to an event and capturing its mood. Writing by hand adds a personal touch.

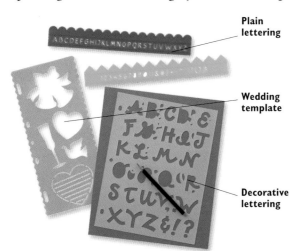

Plain lettering

Wedding template

Decorative lettering

▲ *Plastic templates and stencils are available in a wide range of different styles of lettering and themes.*

▶ *Fibre-tipped pens are easy to use and available in a wide range of colours and widths.*

◀ *Printed journaling blocks can be filled in by hand and then glued on to the album page.*

Templates

Scrapbooking templates in decorative shapes can be used to help you fit and align journaling. Trace one of the shapes on to the page and draw in guidelines with a soft pencil. Rub out the lines when the text is complete. Alternatively, draw round the shape and cut it out of contrasting paper. Add the journaling, erase the guidelines, then glue the paper shape on the layout.

Writing guide

Rest this on the paper and rest your pen lightly on the top of the wire loops as you write. The flexible loops will bend out of the way for the tails of letters descending below the level of the line.

Pens

Fibre-tip pens give good, even coverage. Use the tip for fine writing, and the side to create striking titles.

Fine-tipped pens

Use these when a lot of information has to be written in a small space, as their fine point allows for very neat writing. Fine tips can also be used to decorate titles drawn with thicker pens.

Gel pens

Manufactured in a wide range of colours, gel pens are a scrapbooker's staple. Metallic shades look good on dark paper.

Paint pens

These draw a wide, opaque line of colour, perfect for large titles or for outlining photographs instead of matting.

Computer fonts

A computer will give you access to an almost limitless range of fonts and sizes available for titles and journaling. Titles can be printed out and mounted on a layout, but for a more striking effect, print a title in reverse and cut it out, then flip it over and add to the page. Printing in reverse means any lines will not be seen on the finished layout.

Printed journaling boxes

Sets of journaling boxes offer pre-made titles and sayings to add to a layout, along with some blanks for you to record personal information. These are often produced to coordinate with paper sets, making it easy to complete a layout.

▶ *Fibre-tipped and gel pens are suitable for titles and journaling.*

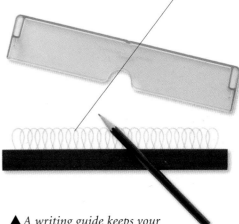

Flexible nylon loops

▲ *A writing guide keeps your handwriting horizontal when journaling without obstructing the movement of the pen.*

Fine-tipped pens

Round-tipped pens

CREATIVE IMAGE-MAKING

Whether you're sorting through boxes of old family pictures or taking new ones with your album in mind, these ideas will help you develop your visual sense and explore imaginative ways of using photographs to create some really arresting images.

Taking good photographs

The craft of scrapbooking sprang from a desire to present photographs of family and friends in a creative and meaningful way, and good photographs are the heart of every album page. So here are some tips to help you take more effective pictures for really stunning layouts. Modern cameras, equipped with high-quality lenses, built-in automatic exposure meters and sophisticated auto-focusing systems, can do nearly all the work for you. Unless you choose to manage your camera's settings manually for creative effects, you really can just point and shoot terrific pictures. However, technical quality is meaningless if your pictures are badly composed, coarsely lit or just lifeless.

Whether you're using a state-of-the-art SLR or a disposable camera, you need to train your eye to make the most of light, colour and form, and learn how to see your subject as the camera sees it to achieve the effective results you want.

Even if you are a good photographer, you are bound to have some pictures that don't come out right, with too much background or foreground, subjects disappearing off the edge of the photo or, if you've used flash, people with red eyes. All is not lost: there are ways of improving many pictures that will enable you to display them.

Photographing people

Whether they're formally posed or candid shots, photographs of people should aim to convey their true character. Most people feel ill-at-ease or put on some kind of show when you first point a lens at them, so it's best to take lots of pictures. Children, especially, will soon forget about the camera's presence if they're busy playing, leaving you to get your best photographs.

For candid shots, a telephoto or zoom lens means your subjects need not be aware of the camera at all. It will also throw the foreground and background out of focus, adding emphasis to the subject, which is just what you want.

Lighting

The traditional instruction to "shoot with the sun behind you" when taking pictures outdoors tends to produce the flattest effect. If your subject is a person looking at the camera, this position will leave them squinting uncomfortably. It can be much more effective to move them into the shade of a tree or a building, where the indirect light will be much more flattering and the contrasts less extreme, making it possible to capture every detail.

If you are taking pictures in direct light, it's best to move yourself or your subject so that the light is coming from one side. This is easiest to achieve when the sun is low in the sky – early in the morning or in the late afternoon (which photographers call the "magic hour"). Indoors, a similar atmospheric sidelight can be provided by daylight coming through a window, which is wonderful for portraits.

Composing pictures

As you look through the viewfinder, or at the LCD screen of a digital camera, it's easy to concentrate too hard on the main subject of your picture, but it's important to see how the whole picture works within the frame. Before you focus and shoot, move the camera around to find the best angle. If necessary, change your position entirely to get a better angle, or to bring in some foreground interest.

Think about the background too: try to find an angle that gives a background that's attractive but not distracting, and look out for ugly details like power lines. If anyone appears to have a tree growing out of their head, move slightly to one side to avoid the problem.

▼ *Here the photographer has successfully used the rule of thirds to make a visually interesting image, but has tilted the camera so that the horizon is not level.*

◀▲ *Red eyes appear when a subject is looking directly at the camera when the flash goes off. The problem is easy to rectify with a red-eye pen. Use it like a felt-tipped pen to mask out the unwanted red tones.*

even remedy pictures that are crooked by cropping a little: draw a new frame parallel with the horizon in the photograph and trim all the edges to produce a straight image.

Red eyes

If people are looking straight at the camera when you take pictures using flash, the light reflects on their retinas, causing their eyes to shine red. Professional photographers use lights set at a distance from the camera to avoid this problem, and some compact cameras that rely on inbuilt flash have a "red-eye reduction" setting, which can help. Another solution is to take pictures when your subjects are not looking directly into the lens.

If you do want to use photographs in which people looking directly at the camera have red eyes, you can improve your prints using a red-eye pen, available from photograhic suppliers. This is a dark green marker pen that successfully counteracts the red, leaving the eyes looking dark. Simply colour in all the red eyes visible on the photograph, taking care not to mark the rest of the faces. The ink is permanent so the colour will not smudge, and your pictures will look much better.

If you're photographing people, move in as close as you can to fill the frame. Alternatively, use a zoom lens – this also has the advantage of flattening the perspective, which has a flattering effect. With children, crouch or kneel to get yourself down to their level.

Try turning the camera on its side. A vertical, or "portrait", format is often better for pictures of people, but that's not always the case. If you're taking the photograph in an interesting setting,

▼*If you forget to check what's going on in the background of a picture while focusing on smiling faces, you can end up with an object appearing to grow out of someone's head.*

including more of the the surroundings in a "landscape" format may convey more information about your subject. For example, you might portray a keen gardener in the context of the garden that they have created.

The most interesting pictures rarely have the main subject right in the centre. Photographers tend to follow the "rule of thirds", which involves visualizing a grid dividing the picture vertically and horizontally into three. Placing your subject on one of the four points where the imaginary lines intersect gives a harmonious composition.

Cropping prints

If you have a photograph where the main focus is too far off to one side, or the subject is set against a busy, distracting background, it is easy to crop the picture to eliminate the unnecessary parts and balance up the composition.

Rather than cutting off the unwanted part of the picture by eye and ending up with a lopsided picture, cut out two L-shaped pieces of black card (card stock). You can use these to form a rectangular frame of any size so that you can judge the part of the picture you want to use. Adjust the L-shapes backwards and forwards until you find the crop that looks best, then mark the print with a pencil. Cut along the marked lines using a craft knife and metal ruler and working on a cutting mat. Cropping pictures will give you a variety of different-sized prints, which can often add interest to album pages. You can

▲ *Everyone has the odd print like this in their collection: most of the sky can simply be cropped away to focus on the main subject.*

▶ *Many badly framed pictures can be redeemed by judicious cropping, but try out your ideas with an adjustable frame, easily made from two pieces of black card, before you start cutting up a print.*

Tinting photographs

Black-and-white photographs, particularly those that have not faded with age, can sometimes look stark in a photograph album. One way to enliven them and give them more interest is to tint them with coloured inks.

I Select the photographs to be hand-tinted. Pour some water mixed with the ink thinner solution into a shallow tray. Using a pair of tweezers, add one photograph at a time to the solution.

2 Place the wet photo on a board and wipe the excess water from it using a cloth. The photo should be damp rather than wet, or the ink will run where the water is rather than where you want it to go.

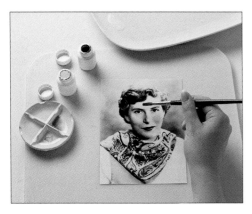

3 Pour a little thinner solution into a palette and add a drop of ink. Apply the colour gently using a fine paintbrush and wait for it to be dispersed by the damp print before adding more. Test the colours to see how different they appear once dry.

4 Add touches of colour to the hair, eyes and lips. Darken the colour as necessary to suit the person in the photograph. Finally, add a few touches of colour to the clothing. Leave the photograph to dry thoroughly before mounting it.

COLOURING MEDIA

Oil-based inks specially formulated for colouring photographs are available in a range of colours and are sold with a thinner solution that can be used to prepare the surface of the print and to dilute the colour. Special marker pens are also available, and can be easier to use for small areas of colour, though the use of a brush can give a more authentic period look. You could also experiment with other media, such as coloured pencils.

The degree to which the colour "takes" will depend on the type of paper used to make the print: if possible select matt prints for colouring as the surface has more grip and will hold the ink more successfully than gloss.

Traditionally, when all photography was in black and white, the most common use for hand-colouring was to add flesh tones to portraits, and doing this will give your prints a period feel. When painting faces, however, take care not to overdo the inking, or your pictures will end up looking like caricatures. If you add too much colour to start with it cannot easily be removed. Use very dilute inks and test all the colours first on a copy of the photograph to ensure that you are happy with the effect and so that you do not risk ruining the original print.

VIRTUAL HAND-TINTING

If you have image-editing software, such as Adobe Photoshop, on your computer, you can apply all kinds of colour effects before making prints. In the example shown here the colourful background was felt to be too dominant and has been selectively converted to black and white so that the album pages stand out more strongly. If you wish to "age" existing black-and-white prints digitally you can scan the images into the computer and add effects such as sepia toning, vignetting or hand-tinting, then print new copies.

Making a photographic mosaic

Try this simple technique to give added interest to an image with bold shapes and colours, or to create an overall pattern from a more detailed picture. Simply cut the print up into a series of small squares and then reassemble it on a coloured background, leaving narrow spaces between the shapes. Mosaic works best on more abstract subjects, or shots of the natural world like these two flower pictures. If you are working with pictures of people, don't make any cuts through the faces as this will alter their proportions.

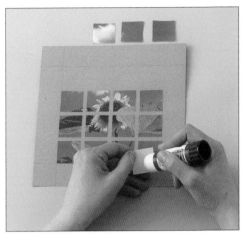

1 Working on a cutting mat, use a clear ruler and a sharp knife to cut the picture into strips of equal width, 2.5–3cm/1–1¼in wide. Cut each strip into squares, keeping them in the correct order as you work to avoid ending up with a jigsaw. A 10 x 15cm/4 x 6in print can be divided into 24 squares each measuring 2.5cm/1in; larger prints can be cut into more squares, or larger squares, as desired.

2 Decide how much space you want around the completed mosaic and how wide to make the distance between the squares. Lightly rule a border on to your chosen backing paper. Starting at the bottom left corner, stick down the first row of squares, making sure that the gaps between them are regular. Continue working upwards until you reach the end of the last row.

3 For a less structured approach, try using a punch to cut out the squares. This method leaves larger, irregular spaces between the picture elements and the finished look resembles a traditional mosaic made from tesserae. Adhesive foam pads add an extra dimension to the finished image. Make sure you are going to punch out a complete square by opening the little flap underneath the cutter and inserting the photograph face down in the punch.

NOW TRY THIS

These two mosaics show complementary variations on the technique. A photograph of russet, gold and green branches takes on an abstract feel when divided into squares, while a picture of rich autumnal foliage provides the perfect frame for a study of a noble tree.

Making a photographic patchwork

Traditional patchwork blocks have a strong geometry, which provides a ready-made framework for floral photographs. Designs such as the hexagonal "Grandmother's Flower Garden" are ideal for showing off your favourite garden pictures, and flowers such as primulas, pansies and apple blossom are reminiscent of the pretty prints on old-fashioned dressmaking fabrics. Look for formal carpet bedding, fields of colourful crops or wild flowers, and take both wide-angle and close-up photographs of them to use in creating your own interpretations of these patterns.

NOW TRY THIS

This bright chequerboard is made up of alternate squares: one a close-up of a poppy flower, the other a wider shot of the field in which it grew. Both pictures were given a pop art look by digitally increasing the contrast and brightness of the original images. The squares butt up to each other so that no background shows through.

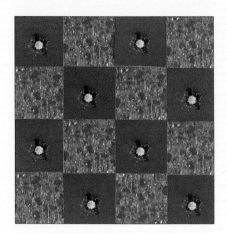

1 Use a patchwork template to cut out a series of hexagons from your prints – you will need to make several copies of each photograph. The centre of each motif is cut from a single close-up and the six hexagons that surround it are made from pictures of massed flowers in a bed.

2 Take time to arrange the shapes before sticking them down, making sure that you have enough of each type. Starting at the bottom left corner, glue six patterned hexagons around a plain coloured one. Leaving a 6mm/¼in space all around, make more interlocking motifs to fill the page. Trim the edges flush with the background.

Weaving photographic images

This technique requires planning, but the results are well worth it and often produce unexpected effects. Experiment by combining a black-and-white and a coloured copy of the same photograph to create extra depth, as shown with the picture of a Japanese news stand, or by weaving an abstract photograph of texture with a landscape. Weaving works best on landscape or abstract images: as with photographic mosaics, avoid using close-up portraits.

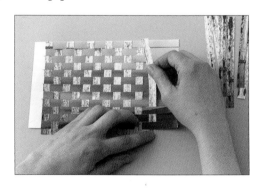

1 For a square weave, cut the black-and-white version of the picture into horizontal strips 2cm/¾in wide, stopping just short of one end so that they remain joined together. Use a sharp knife and a transparent ruler, and work carefully on a cutting mat. Cut the coloured picture into separate vertical strips of the same width.

2 Weave the first strip from the left of the coloured picture under and over the black-and-white strips. Take the second strip and weave it under the alternate strips: repeat this to the end, making sure that they are all at right angles and that the space between them is minimal. Secure the ends of the strips with double-sided tape and display the finished piece in a window mount.

3 To create a basket weave, in which the horizontal strips form rectangles and the vertical ones squares, leave a 3mm/⅛in gap between the short strips. Two very different pictures – one of a stunning coastal sunset and the other of a rusting iron shed – are combined in this weave. They work well together because they have very similar colour schemes.

Making panoramas and compositions

Panoramic cameras are fun to use but you don't actually need one to make your own panorama. If you take two or more photographs from the same viewpoint, turning the camera slightly each time, you can then trim and stick the photographs together to make a long, narrow view. You can also use variations on this technique to create extended panoramas from just a single image or use your imagination to combine different images, with surprising results.

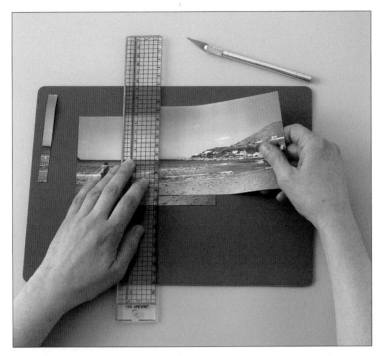

▲ If you are making a joined panorama remember that photographs tend be slightly darker towards the edges (a natural consequence of producing a rectangular image with a round lens) so it's best not to butt untrimmed vertical edges together. Instead, overlap the pictures to see how much of the image they share, then trim half this width from one picture. Put them together with the trimmed photo on top, align a ruler with the trimmed edge, slide away the top picture and trim the bottom one.

▲ Turn a single portrait-format view into an extended landscape, or composite panorama, by combining two identical prints. Cut strips of varying width from each side of one photograph and mount them either side of your main image. If you leave narrow spaces between them, it is less obvious that they simply repeat the image rather than extending it.

▲ An interesting variation on the composite panorama is to use two very different but related pictures to encapsulate memories of an event or place. Here a photograph of a Greek flag is interspersed with a geometric abstract view of buildings clinging to the steep hillside of the Cycladic island of Syros. Staggering the strips adds to the geometric nature of the images.

▲ A quick way to join two similar pictures is to find an obvious vertical line or strong outline along the edge of one of them and cut along it. You can then overlay this edge across the other picture. Although the two pictures used here were not taken from the same spot, they share the same colours and tonal range, so give the effect of two people appearing in the same photograph.

▲ *A great way to produce a multifaceted image of an event or scene is as a photo-composite, in the style of artist David Hockney. To do this, take lots of pictures from different angles and combine them in a collage. This view of the lake and Palm House at the Royal Botanic Gardens in Kew, London, includes several photographs of the same pair of swans, creating the illusion of a larger flock.*

Transferring photographs on to fabric

Several types of special paper are available for transferring photographs on to fabric. Your pictures will not be damaged by the process but it must be undertaken at a photocopy bureau. Copy several photographs together on to one sheet. Make sure you have enough transfers to allow for experimentation and mistakes. Some photographs do not work well on transfer paper, such as those with dark backgrounds or lots of contrast, so be prepared for some trial and error.

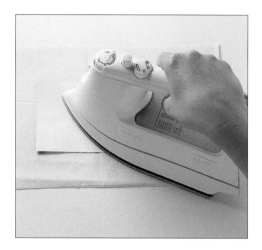

1 Stick the photographs lightly on to a piece of plain paper. Take this to a colour copy bureau together with the transfer paper, which needs to be fed one sheet at a time through the paper tray. (Have the photographs copied using a normal colour process to check the colour before they are copied on to the transfer paper.) Trim around a transfer and place it face down on a plain natural fabric with a close weave, such as calico, which will withstand heat and pressure. Referring to the manufacturer's instructions, press with a hot iron. If a lot of pressure is required, it may be advisable to work on a sturdy table protected with several layers of blanket.

2 Carefully peel off the transfer backing in an even movement to reveal the transferred image. Allow the fabric to cool before using it. Refer to the transfer paper manufacturer's instructions for washing and aftercare. A more expensive, but generally foolproof method of photo transfer is to have the process done professionally at a copy bureau that prints T-shirts with your own images.

NOW TRY THIS

This endearing photograph of a much-loved pet required special treatment. The image was transferred on to a piece of natural linen and the vintage-style fabric that forms the frame was carefully selected to echo the paisley quilt the kitten is sitting on. A narrow lace edging and pearl buttons complete the frame.

NOW TRY THIS

This sophisticated cloth book would make a wonderful keepsake for a young child. Take close-up photographs of familiar scenes around the child's house and garden and transfer them on to a coarsely woven fabric such as linen or calico to give them a canvas-like texture. Trim each one to 12.5cm/5in square and tack (baste) it to a 16.5 x 18cm/6½ x 7in felt rectangle, allowing a 2cm/¾in border around three sides and a wider border at the spine. Attach with a decorative machine stitch, then assemble the pages and stitch along the spine. You could also embellish the pages with embroidered messages, printed text or other appliquéd decoration.

Making a kaleidoscope

The multi-faceted image inside a kaleidoscope is created by reflecting an image between two angled mirrors to produce a repeating, symmetrical pattern. With patience it is possible to make your own photographic version: the effect is stunning, complex, and can be slightly surreal, as with this reinterpretation of a Venetian canal scene. You will need eight prints of the same picture, four of them reversed.

1 Draw a square on acetate or tracing paper and divide it diagonally to make a triangular template. Cut it out and use to make two sets of four triangles from the photographs. Clear acetate will enable you to position the template accurately so that the images are identical, with one set a mirror image of the other.

2 Mark a square sheet of paper into eight equal sections: these will be your guidelines for assembling the pattern. Matching the sides of the images exactly, glue the segments in place, making sure that each one lies next to its mirror image.

3 You can then trim the finished pattern as you wish: into a square, a four-point star or, as here, a circle. Mark the circumference with a pair of compasses and cut around the pencil line.

4 If you choose an image that is already symmetrical you can make a kaleidoscope from four, six or eight prints without having to reverse them. Here, the iconic image of the Eiffel Tower is surrounded by pictures of a period shop front to create a unique souvenir of Paris.

NOW TRY THIS

Here, eight diamonds form the design known in patchwork as the LeMoyne Star, giving the original flower image an abstract quality.

Framing and mounting photographs

There are many possible ways to frame your favourite photographs and cards. All the ideas shown here are quick and easy to do and look very effective, both in album pages and as fresh ways of displaying photographs in frames. Try them on your own layouts, or use them as inspiration for your original ideas.

CUTTING PAPER FRAMES

Single or multiple borders in paper or thin card (stock), known as mats, are a simple way to present a picture, but must be accurately cut for successful results. Choose colours that match or contrast effectively with the dominant colours in the photographs, and make sure that each successive border balances the photograph and is evenly positioned around the picture.

▲ *On this album page attention is focused on a single image by mounting it in a double mat in two colours. The opening in the top layer is cut a little larger to expose a narrow contrasting inner border.*

▲ *In this charming treatment the paper border is arranged some way away from the edge of the photograph, so that the background acts as an inner frame. A spray of die-cut daisies completes the effect.*

▲ *Multiple paper frames in a simple colour scheme are a great way to give unity to a diverse collection of photographs and other memorabilia. Extra layers can be added to disguise differences of size.*

▼ *For this stacked technique the subject is cut out first and used as the template for the border shapes, each drawn 6mm/^{1}/$_4$in larger than the layer above. The careful choice of graduated tones, complementing the bird's plumage, gives a subtle three-dimensional effect.*

▲ *Here the background colour matches the vehicle, and contrast is provided by the square black frames, each of which has a window a little larger than the cut-out photograph, leaving a striking band of colour around each picture.*

USING TEMPLATES

Plastic templates are available in a host of different shapes and sizes, from simple geometric forms to outlines of cats and Christmas trees. You can also draw and cut your own from many sources. Basic shapes such as ovals are useful guides for trimming photographs accurately, and are easy to use.

1 Position a template over the part of the photograph you want to use and draw around the outline with a pencil.

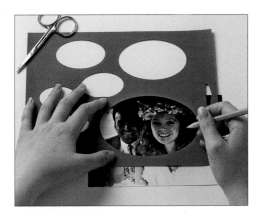

2 Use a small, sharp pair of scissors to cut carefully around the pencil line.

▲ *Use a set of templates in graduated sizes to cut a series of mats or frames to fit around your picture.*

1 Cut out a narrow frame from a photograph with a lot of background to draw attention to the focal point.

2 Turn the cut-out section by 45 degrees and replace it between the central area and the border to complete the frame.

▲ *Alternatively, cut away the outer sections of the picture in regular shapes, then offset them slightly and glue to a backing sheet.*

▲ *For a rainbow effect, use a template to cut a succession of circles, then offset them.*

▲ *Make a frame to suit your subject, like this porthole for an underwater theme.*

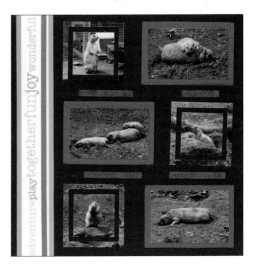

▲ *Different framing methods are unified here by consistent use of colour and shape.*

TEARING PAPER FRAMES

Torn paper shapes can add softness and a change of texture to your layouts, but it's a good idea to use the effect sparingly, as it can easily become too dominant. Combine it with neat, straight edges for contrast, or make a mosaic of lots of small-scale torn edges using different colours for a subtle collage.

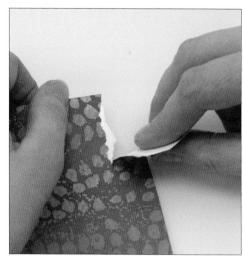

I Tearing paper or card (stock) that is coloured the same shade all through gives a soft textured edge. The feathery lines are good for recreating textures such as teddy bear fur, or for layering to create backgrounds resembling water, clouds or grass. Tearing with the grain of the paper gives a straighter edge than tearing against the grain, so practise to see the effects you can achieve. To make it easier to tear a shape, try drawing with a dampened paintbrush along the line you want to tear.

2 Patterned paper is usually printed and has a white core. Tearing the paper will reveal this. Tearing towards yourself with the pattern uppermost produces a white edge, which highlights the tear. If you don't want to make a feature of this, tear the paper from the other side so that the rough white edge is concealed under the printed top layer. This is a good choice when you want to create a softer line, perhaps when overlapping torn edges to create a change of colour.

▲ *A sheet of torn mulberry paper in a toning colour makes a lovely textural border for a picture. Tearing this paper pulls out the fibres to make a softly fringed edge. The paper should be dampened where you want it to part. For a straight tear, fold it and wet the folded edge then gently pull it apart. For the more random tearing used here, dampen the paper by drawing curves and shapes with a wet paintbrush or cotton bud (swab).*

DECORATING PAPER FRAMES

You can use pre-printed stickers, but it is easy to make your own frames to suit a particular theme. Trace motifs from books or magazines on to plain paper and adjust the scale on a photocopier if necessary to make a template. Draw around or trace the design on to coloured paper and cut out as many shapes as you need, then glue them on to your album page.

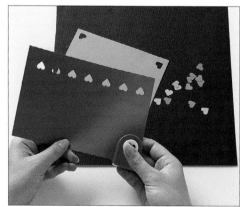

▲ *Specially shaped edging scissors are available in many different designs, and you can use these to create smart decorative effects on coloured paper frames.*

▲ *You can decorate the corners of frames with a punched motif, or punch rows of decorative holes all round the edge. Keep the shapes to decorate the rest of the album page.*

▲ *Use a template to cut decorative shapes from appropriately coloured paper to highlight the theme of an album page, and let them overlap the picture frames.*

▲ *Create an informal look by making a frame from printed stickers. Mount the photograph on a plain background then mass the stickers in groups around it, overlapping the edges and each other.*

▲ *A pricked design makes a pretty, lacy edging for a simple paper frame. Draw the design lightly in pencil then prick evenly along the lines with a bodkin, resting the frame on a soft surface such as a cork tile.*

▲ *Use a stamp of a frame and bright ink to make a frame on plain coloured paper. Cut out a wavy edge for a funky look.*

NOW TRY THIS

Instead of framing pictures, try mounting them over blocks of bright colour to create a collage effect, then frame them with groups of flowers in co-ordinating shades. These could be stickers or your own photographs, carefully cut out.

1 Select individual flowerheads to match the colours in your pictures and cut them out, carefully eliminating any background.

2 Arrange the coloured paper shapes for the background and glue in place, then position the photographs.

3 Arrange the flower cut-outs to create a scattered effect over the background areas, co-ordinating the colours and allowing the petals to overlap the edges of the photographs.

BACKGROUND TREATMENTS

Rather than have plain backgrounds to the pages in your album, decorate them with stamps, stencils, stickers and paint effects in colours and themes that are sympathetic to your photographs. Choose subdued, muted shades for subtle compositions, or be more adventurous and experiment with unusual combinations of colour and pattern.

Choosing colours

The background should flatter the photographs rather than overpower them and its style needs to be in keeping with the subject matter. But you need not restrict your choice to a single colour or design: try making up collages of interesting textures and patterns. Include greetings cards, wrapping paper, children's artwork, and even fabric swatches.

▲ *Once you have decided on the images you want to mount, think about colours and motifs that underline their theme. These gold papers suit a wedding layout and the heart is a traditional symbol. Play around with combinations of papers until you find a good balance between images and background.*

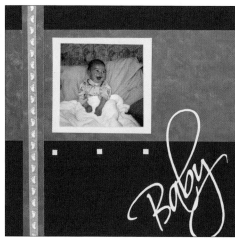

▲ *Blue is the traditional colour scheme for a baby boy, but the dark blue background overlaid with simple bands of lighter tones, with only tiny dashes of baby blue, give this simple treatment a modern look.*

▲ *Do not shy away from patterned backgrounds; these scraps of delicately patterned wallpaper work beautifully with each other and the warm tones of the cat.*

▲ *If you place the same images on a different background, with colours that clash with the photographs, you can instantly see that it is an unsuitable combination.*

COMPLEMENTARY COLOURS

1 Allow the photographs to dictate your choice of background colours, rather than choosing a paper and hoping the pictures will match it. Hold your images against a wide variety of colours and patterns before making your choice. Here the photograph is overpowered by the colour of the background paper.

2 Orange and green are opposite each other on the colour wheel, so they complement each other well and the cooler colour tends to recede, making the picture of the pumpkins stand out as the focal point. Against this background you could use accents of orange and other warm, toning colours such as peach and gold to accompany the image.

Using patterns

Patterned backgrounds help to give layouts a distinctive style, but need to be carefully chosen to avoid dominating the images and other elements that you may choose to add to the page. Make sure the colours and contrasts in the photographs are strong enough to stand out from the background.

MONOCHROME SCHEMES

An easy way to begin experimenting with pattern is to restrict your use of colour.

1 Gather together a selection of papers, patterned and plain, in a single colour. Experiment by overlapping them or placing them next to each other until you find an arrangement you like. Choose one as the background, and cut a few rectangles or strips from the other papers.

2 For this layout, cut a rectangle of plain blue paper 18 × 25cm/7 × 10in and a strip 5 × 30cm/2 × 12in from another pattern. Stick the rectangle to the left-hand side of the page, 2.5cm/1in in from the top, bottom and left side. Arrange the patterned strip horizontally across the page so it overlaps the lower part of the rectangle. Mat the photographs and add them to the layout.

▲ *Using the same design in a different colour scheme and with different subjects changes the look entirely. Here, the monochromatic green layout includes touches of pale yellow in the flower and buttons to pick up the yellow details in the photographs.*

COMBINING PATTERNED PAPERS

Many ranges of patterned paper are specially designed to be used in combination, making it easy to create interesting backgrounds.

1 This design mimics a wall with wallpaper and a dado rail, the perfect place to display a few photos. Choose a 30cm/12in square sheet of paper for the background and cut a strip of another paper 10cm/4in wide.

2 Glue the strip to the bottom of the page and cover the join with a length of toning ribbon. Arrange two large photographs on the upper part of the page. With a button and an extra length of ribbon, suspend a smaller photo from the ribbon "rail".

▲ *These two papers harmonize perfectly because although the patterns contrast in shape and scale they are printed in the same range of colours. When mixing patterns, go for colours in the same tonal family and try teaming stripes with floral designs, or look for the same motifs in different sizes.*

USING STRIPES AS BORDERS

If you are combining striped and patterned paper, the stripes can be cut up to form a border around the page and frames for the photographs.

1 Choose a paper with wide stripes, and cut four identical strips 4 x 30cm/1½ x 12in. Mount one on each side of the page, matching the stripes. Glue another along the bottom and mitre the corners by cutting diagonally through both layers.

2 Add the last strip at the top of the page, making sure the strips correspond as before, and mitre the two top corners. Mat your selection of photographs in toning shades and mount on the page.

▲ *Four black-and-white photographs of disparate subjects are neatly unified with this simple treatment, which does not distract attention from the pictures.*

USING BOLD PATTERNS

Some patterned papers are bold and dramatic but won't overwhelm photographs if they are paired with strong images or colours. Close-ups of faces or objects work best.

1 Choose a patterned paper that includes as many of the colours in your choice of photographs as possible. Here the bright pinks and oranges pick up the colours of the flowers and the vivid stripes convey the exuberance of spring blossom.

2 Pick shades from the patterned paper to mat the photos: this will help them stand out from the background. Add embellishments that match the colour and theme of the layout.

▶ *The pretty ribbons on this page are chosen to match the striped paper, while the little flower buttons echo the springtime theme.*

Collage techniques

Building up a multi-layered background using different papers allows you to introduce a satisfying variety of texture and colour.

USING MULBERRY PAPER

Mulberry paper is available plain or printed, and some sheets incorporate pieces of flowers or leaves, making perfect backgrounds for pictures with a pastoral or garden theme. Its soft feathered edges are very attractive.

1 Choose a selection of papers that match the tones of the photograph. Strips of paper will be used to extend the bands of colour in the sky. To tear them, dip a paintbrush in water then trace a line on the paper. Pull the paper apart while it is wet.

2 Build up the scene with torn strips of mulberry paper; a different shade is created when two colours of the paper overlap. Mat the photograph in black, so that its straight edges form a striking contrast with the soft outlines of the mulberry paper, and mount it on the background.

▲ *This lovely photograph of a sunset has an almost abstract quality, and the collage background made with torn strips of mulberry paper extends the scene very effectively. The dark foreground, reduced to a silhouette in the fading light, is matched by a sheet of black paper covering the lower part of the page.*

MAKING A PAPER COLLAGE

Subtle colour effects can be achieved by building up small pieces of torn paper in a range of toning colours. Begin by tearing a good quantity of the colours you need before applying any glue.

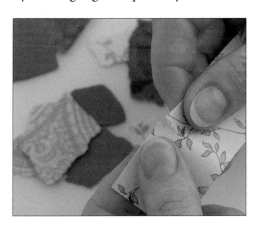

1 Tear the paper into small pieces of a fairly even size, aiming to make rounded shapes. Tear away the straight edges of the paper so that they are roughly torn on all sides.

2 Glue the pieces to the background in a group, overlapping them and mixing the colours at random. If you want to create the effect of falling leaves, you could add a scattering of isolated pieces.

3 Add details to the collage if you wish by stamping motifs or drawing them in with a fibre-tipped pen in a toning colour.

▶ *Here a photograph is enhanced by a colour-co-ordinated collage in subdued colours that has been aged with stamping.*

USING COLLAGED PAPER

Some patterned papers have a collage-effect design, with elements scattered across the paper. If you cut around parts of these, you can slide photographs underneath to look as if they are part of the overall design.

1 Mark with a pencil where a corner or edge of the photograph intersects with an element in the pattern. Use a craft knife to trim along the edge of the pattern.

2 Make more slits across the page to accommodate the photographs you wish to include. Mat the photos and slide them under the flaps.

▲ *Single elements, such as the suitcase on this travel-themed layout, can be trimmed from another sheet of patterned paper and added as embellishments.*

COLOUR BLOCKING

This is an easy technique to master, especially for beginners and when using a monochromatic colour scheme. Photographs and other elements can sit neatly within one block or overlap across several. This design for a 30cm/12in album page is based on a grid of 8 x 8 squares.

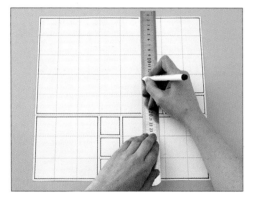

1 Using a grid of 4cm/1½in squares, design the blocks for your layout.

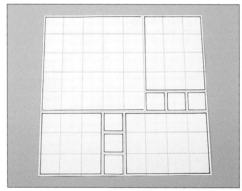

2 Rule 6mm/¼in margins between the blocks and all round the edge of the sheet.

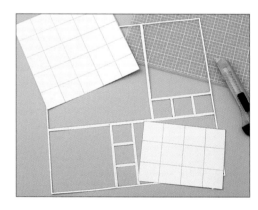

3 Use a craft knife and ruler to cut each template piece out of the grid.

4 Draw round each template on the back of patterned paper and cut out. Use a different paper for each section.

5 Glue the cut-out papers on to a background sheet of 30cm/12in card (stock), following the original layout.

6 Add photographs, embellishments and journaling as desired.

Traditional patchwork patterns include lots of designs that can be adapted to scrapbooking. This one is called "Shoo Fly" and is a simple combination of squares and triangles in a balanced design to which photographs can be added.

1 Choose one 30cm/12in square paper for the background. From a different paper, cut three 10cm/4in squares. Cut two of these in half diagonally.

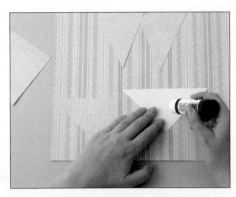

2 Position the background square centrally on the page, and arrange one triangle diagonally across each corner. Glue in place.

3 Add lines of "stitching" around the patches with a black pen to mimic running stitch and oversew stitch. Glue the remaining square in the centre.

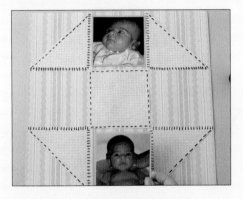

4 Arrange the photographs and embellishments between the patches.

◀ *The patchwork theme is enhanced with drawn-in stitching and lettering designed to resemble appliqué.*

MAKING A SILHOUETTE

This makes an interesting treatment for a photograph of someone in profile. Cut the profile out of black or coloured card (card stock) to form an accompaniment to the photo. You can use the photograph as your guide for the silhouette, or you could draw your own version.

1 Using a computer or photocopier, enlarge the photograph to the desired size for the silhouette and glue to a sheet of dark card.

2 Cut carefully around the outline of the person in the print using a pair of sharp-pointed scissors.

3 Reverse the silhouette and add it to the layout, positioning it to balance the original photograph.

Adding paint, chalk and ink

Instead of using printed paper, you can create your own unique patterns to form tailor-made backgrounds for your collections. If you don't feel confident about your painting and drawing skills, just choose from the host of ready-made stencils and stamps available, and work with colour-washed backgrounds.

PAINTING BACKGROUNDS

For interesting textural effects, make patterns in wet paint. You can try a variety of objects such as the blunt end of a paintbrush, a cocktail stick (toothpick) or a wooden skewer, drawing simple curls, spirals and stars. Or cut a comb from stiff cardboard and draw it through the paint.

1 Mix some acrylic paint with wallpaper paste to make a thick paste. With a wide brush, paint the surface of a sheet of heavy cartridge (construction) paper using even strokes in one direction. Use a comb to make patterns in the wet paint.

2 Draw the comb in two directions for a woven pattern, or use random strokes for bark-like effects. Allow the paper to dry completely. If it buckles, press the back with a cool iron, then leave it between heavy books to keep it flat.

ANTIQUING

Paper with an aged look can be useful for heritage layouts, either as a background, as part of a collage, or for titles and journaling.

1 To achieve an antique effect, brush a strong solution of tea over the surface of white paper. Allow to dry, then press with a cool iron if necessary to flatten. The paper can then be torn or cut up to use in a collage. You could also try singeing the edges to add to the effect.

RUBBER STAMPING

There are literally hundreds of rubber stamps available on the market nowadays, so you will always be able to find something to complement your album page designs. You could use small motifs for surface decoration, or large scale designs that form an all-over background pattern.

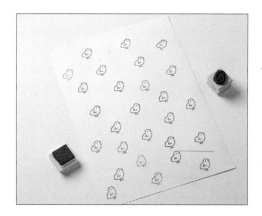

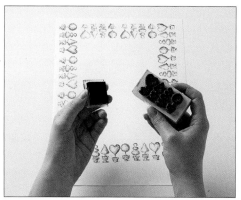

1 Use a single motif to stamp an all-over design on to plain paper to create a patterned background. Press the stamp in the ink pad, then press it on the paper, taking care not to smudge. Repeat as desired. Apply the images in a random pattern, or rule faint pencil guidelines.

2 The elongated shape of this topiary stamp makes it ideal for a border design. If you want a symmetrical design, measure the stamp and work out how many repeats will fit the page. Ensure the stamp aligns with the edge, and that each new print lines up with the designs already stamped.

3 Rubber-stamped designs can be enhanced very simply by colouring the motifs lightly with coloured pencils. You could also try using various kinds of paint to achieve different effects.

USING CHALKS

Sets of acid-free chalks are available in various ranges of different shades and can be used to create very soft colour effects on very light or very dark papers. To extend the tones of a photograph across a full layout, use chalks to recreate the scene, or use them to tint embossed paper.

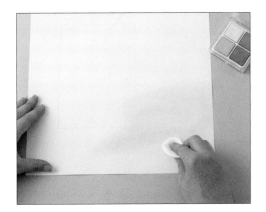

1 Measure the photograph, subtract 1cm/⅜in from each side, and trace the dimensions on to a 30cm/12in square sheet of white card (stock). With a pad of cotton wool (ball), pick up some coloured chalk and rub it across the page.

2 Continue to build up the chalk scene, matching the shades used in the photograph and using a clean pad for each new colour. For details such as the path and fence posts, use a cotton bud (swab) or the applicator supplied with the chalk to draw finer lines.

3 Leave the page overnight, to allow the chalks to settle into the paper. Finally, add the photograph in the marked area.

COMBINING CHALKS AND STAMPING

Used together, rubber stamps and chalks enable you to combine fine pictorial detail with soft colouring. You can either use the chalks to fill in the stamped motifs or rub them over the paper to create a mist of colour over the whole page before applying the stamped image.

1 Choose rubber stamp motifs to match the theme of the page and stamp them at random over the background sheet using a range of coloured inks. Using a cotton wool pad (ball) rub chalks in toning colours across the page to create a soft wash of background colour. Leave the page for a few hours to allow the chalk to settle into the paper, then add the matted photographs and embellishments.

▶ *The smaller photograph of a leafy country track inspired the choice of leaf stamps in soft autumn shades for this background. The chalks harmonize well with the horse's colouring, and a length of real ribbon provides the finishing touch.*

STENCILLING

Charming backgrounds can be created using stencils, which work well with paints, oil sticks or chalks. Stencils are easy to cut from manila card or clear acetate, and you can work from templates or draw your own. Hundreds of ready-cut designs are also available in craft stores.

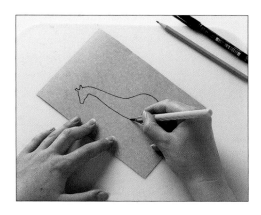

1 Trace the design and transfer it to stencil card. Working on a cutting mat and using a craft knife cut out each shape, taking care not to cut through any "bridges" holding elements of the design in place.

2 Using an oil stick or appropriate paint, and a large stencil brush, dab paint on to the chosen area using the stencil. Lift the stencil carefully to avoid smudging the edges and leave to dry.

3 Add details with a second stencil. Leave to dry.

▼ *Stencilled animals and a Noah's ark make a lovely setting for a young child's picture.*

EMBELLISHING THE PAGES

Adding the final decorative touches is often the most enjoyable part of assembling your album pages. The elements you use should enhance the photographs and complement the background.

Papercraft

Keep a collection of offcuts of interesting papers for these delicate decorations, which use precise folding and cutting to create pretty three-dimensional ornaments, from decorative tags and envelopes to classic origami flowers.

▲ *The photographs here have been enhanced with rolled paper frames.*

PAPER ROLLING

Rolled paper edgings and frames work particularly well when you use paper that is printed differently on each side, as the rolling exposes the contrasting pattern or colour.

1 To create a rolled heart, draw the shape on the back of the paper and cut a series of slashes from the centre to the edge.

2 Roll a dampened cotton bud (swab) along the cut edges to soften the fibres. Turn the paper over and roll each section towards the edge of the shape.

3 Glue a photograph or embellishment in the centre of the heart motif.

MAKING A LACÉ DESIGN

Pronounced "lassay", this technique works best when cut from two-sided card (stock). It can be cut using a metal template (you can buy lots of different designs) or you can devise your own using a pair of compasses or a protractor. Small patterned cuts are made in the card and the cut piece is bent over to form a bicoloured design.

1 Transfer the template to the wrong side of the card using a pencil (the lines will be erased later).

2 Using a sharp craft knife, cut neatly along the lines from end to middle. Erase the pencil marks and turn the card over.

3 Lift one petal and fold it backwards. Once all the petals are folded, tuck each one under the edge of the previous point.

PAPER APPLIQUÉ

Appliqué literally means "applied". Usually appliqué is a technique used with fabric in the art of patchwork. Here it is used with paper. Cut-out shapes in paper or card (stock) of different colours or patterns can be layered together to create three-dimensional motifs. Here the appliqué effect is emphasized by lines of decorative "stitches" drawn around the card patches. Attaching the motif by means of sticky foam pads raises it a little above the surface, so that the butterfly seems to hover over the flowers.

1 Trace the outlines of the butterfly and the applied panels for the wings and copy them on to a sheet of card to make templates. Cut out all the pieces.

2 Select sheets of card in four different colours. Draw round the templates for the basic shape and the body in one colour, and divide the smaller coloured details between the remaining sheets, keeping the design symmetrical.

3 Cut out all the pieces of the butterfly.

4 Using a fine-tipped black pen, draw lines of small "stitches" around the edge of each coloured shape. Glue the shapes to the butterfly's wings. Create a pair of antennae from a length of fine silver wire, curling the ends tightly, and glue to the head. Attach the body to the wings using foam pads to give a three-dimensional effect, and use more foam pads to anchor the butterfly to the background.

▶ *This cut-out butterfly, floating a little above the surface of the album page, softens what would otherwise be a very rigid layout of squares, and is perfectly in keeping with the floral theme. The colours of the panels on its wings are repeated in the picture mats.*

QUILLING

Thin strips of finely rolled paper are arranged into pictorial images suitable for scrapbooking. This traditional craft requires a special tool and narrow strips of plain coloured paper, which you can buy specially cut. It is possible to cut them yourself but they must be precisely the same width all along their length. Once you've mastered your first roll (it's very easy) you can make this pretty flower.

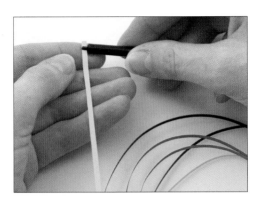

I Make the leaves first. Slide one end of a green strip into the notch on the quilling tool.

2 Roll the paper tightly and evenly on to the tool.

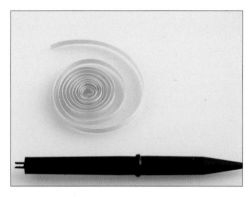

3 Gently ease the rolled paper off the tool and allow it to uncoil to the desired size. Glue the end and hold until dry.

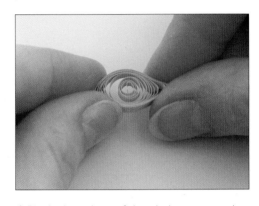

4 Pinch the edges of the circle on opposite sides, using your thumbs and forefingers.

5 Make four red coils for the petals. Make two pinches close to each other, and press the rest of the circle down towards them.

6 Roll a tight black coil for the centre. Cut a stem from green paper and assemble the pieces to complete the poppy.

DECORATING TAGS

Tags are quick-to-make scrapbook embellishments and use only small quantities of materials. You can use a die-cutting machine or templates, or make the shape by just snipping the corners off a rectangle.

I Snip two corners off a rectangle of card. Punch a hole for the string and shape the other two corners with a corner cutter.

2 Embellish the tag as desired. In this case ribbons and ribbon roses were used and the tag was tied with coloured fibres.

▲ *Use simple tags to hold pictures or text, or just as decoration. They can be glued to a page or hung by ribbon ties.*

MAKING POCKETS

As vellum is translucent, you can use this simple pocket for photos, or just slip some journaling or souvenirs such as tickets inside.

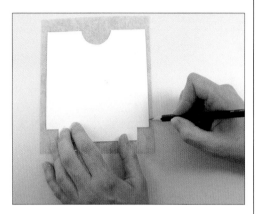

1 Cut out a pocket template and draw around it on vellum.

2 Fold in the side and bottom flaps. Glue the flaps and attach to the layout.

▼ *Vellum allows you to see what's inside the pocket without taking it out.*

MAKING MINI-ENVELOPES

A tiny envelope adds excitement to a page, and could be used to hold small treasures such as a handful of confetti in a wedding album, a scrap of lace or even a lock of hair. Or you could inscribe a secret message on a little card and tuck it inside.

1 Draw around an envelope template and cut out.

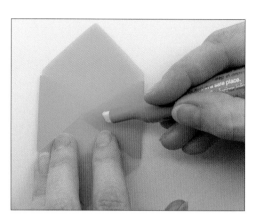

2 Fold in three of the corners and glue the overlapping edges. Fold down the top.

▶ *For a page celebrating the arrival of a baby girl, you could decorate some little envelopes with pretty labels and tiny pink bows.*

PLASTIC POCKETS

Cut a pocket from the lower edge of a stationery folder. Staple the sides together and insert a memento. Staple the top closed or leave it open so that the contents can be taken out.

Cut two squares from a plastic folder and pierce holes around the edges. Attach a memento or decorations to one piece using double-sided tape. Lace the sides together with cord and knot the ends.

MAKING POP-UP PAGES

Proper pop-ups like these party balloons work only on pages that aren't in page protectors, since it's the action of the pages opening out that makes the pop-up rise. You can, however, arrange lifting flaps on single pages inside page protectors, either by cutting a slit for them or by sticking them to the outside with another, cut-down, page protector to cover them. These pages are good for children's themes.

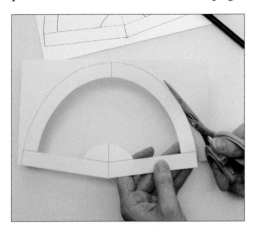

1 Transfer the pop-up template at the back of the book to white card (stock) and cut it out. Score along the dotted lines. Fold the bottom struts up and the arch back.

▼*A pop-up is a dramatic ornament for a strap or post-bound album.*

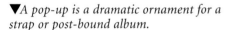

2 Apply adhesive to the bottom of the two struts, then glue the whole pop-up in place across two pages of the album. Following the templates, cut out the four balloons and two presents from plain card in a range of bright colours.

3 Wrap a ribbon round each present and tie ribbons round the ends of the balloons. Stick the parcels on the base of the pop-up, and balloons on the arch, making sure they will not jam the pop-up when it closes. Stick the tails of the balloons behind the parcels. Add photographs to the layout.

TEABAG FOLDING

This technique gets its unusual name because its inventor made her first fold using a colourful teabag envelope. It's also known as miniature kaleidoscopic origami, and you can buy or download sheets printed with small patterned squares. The easiest design is a rosette, which can be used as a decorative element or as the "O" in a word like "snow" or "love".

1 Cut out eight patterned teabag squares from a printed sheet.

2 Fold the first square diagonally, with the patterned side inside.

3 Unfold and turn the paper over so the back of the square is facing you.

4 Fold the square in half horizontally, taking the bottom edge up to the top edge.

5 Unfold it, then fold it in half vertically, taking the right edge to the left edge with the patterned side outside. Unfold.

6 With the patterned side facing you, push the valley folds in and bring the two uncreased quarters of the square together.

7 Fold all the remaining squares in the same way, then take one in your fingers, with the peak down and the open folds to the top.

8 Open the fold on one side, and spread some glue on it. Slide the next square, peak down, in between these two sticky sides, and press to make the glue stick.

9 Go round the circle, adding each square in the same way until the rosette is complete, then glue the last section over the first.

▲ *Adding green paper stems and simple leaf shapes to these teabag rosettes turns them into stylized flowers to decorate a layout with a garden theme.*

10 Glue a cluster of beads or sequins in the centre to complete the decoration.

IRIS FOLDING

This technique creates intricate spiralling designs using folded strips of paper arranged like the panels of a camera iris. It is an ingenious method of creating curved forms using only straight components, and looks very effective when mounted inside an aperture. Experiment with combinations of plain and patterned paper or contrasting colours.

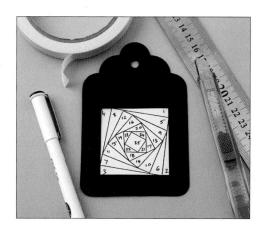

3 Cut a 5cm/2in aperture in black card (stock) and use low-tack masking tape to fix the template temporarily within the aperture. The pattern will be built up backwards, so place the black card face down on the table, with the template below.

1 Choose four different shades of paper and cut into strips 2cm/¾in wide.

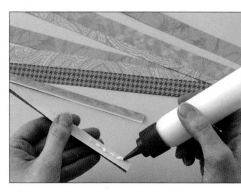

2 Fold each strip in half lengthways and glue the two sides together, right sides out.

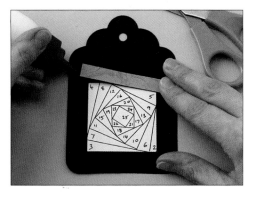

4 Cut a piece 6cm/2¼in long from a length of brown paper. Line it up to cover the triangle labelled 1, with the folded edge towards the centre. Glue the edges of the strip to stick it down (be careful not to get any adhesive on the template below).

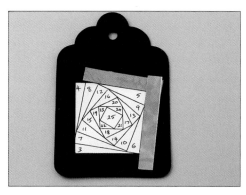

5 Take a 6cm/2¼in length of pink paper, and glue it in position to cover the section marked 2 on the template.

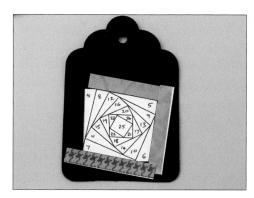

6 Take a 6cm/2¼in length of blue paper, and glue it in position to cover the section marked 3 on the template.

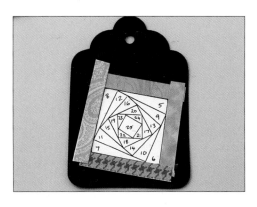

7 Take a 6cm/2¼in length of green paper, and glue it in position to cover the section marked 4 on the template.

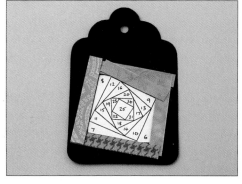

8 Continue round the spiral, adding paper strips as follows: brown (5), pink (6), blue (7), green (8), brown (9), pink (10), blue (11), green (12), brown (13), pink (14), blue (15), green (16), brown (17), pink (18), blue (19), green (20), brown (21), pink (22) blue (23), green (24).

9 The strips spiral into the centre, leaving a square hole (section 25 on the template).

▲ *This six-petalled flower design accentuates the spiralling shapes created in iris folding. This time just three different papers have been used, and a paper stem and leaves have been added to complete the picture.*

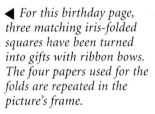

◄ *For this birthday page, three matching iris-folded squares have been turned into gifts with ribbon bows. The four papers used for the folds are repeated in the picture's frame.*

10 Cover the central hole by gluing on a square of brown paper.

11 Turn the card over and remove the template to reveal the completed design.

12 Turn the square into a house with a brown triangle for the roof and a folded paper chimney.

Adding metal and wire

Eyelets, wire decorations and metal tags add lustre and a change of texture to your layouts. Make sure hard materials of this kind are well protected and positioned so that they will not damage your precious photographs.

EMBOSSING METAL

Foil of around 38 gauge is suitable for embossing, working on the back to create a raised pattern, or on the front to indent a pattern.

1 To make a tag, draw round a card tag on a sheet of foil using an embossing tool or dry ballpoint pen and a ruler.

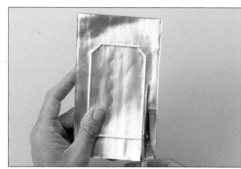

2 Cut out the tag with old scissors, trimming 2mm/¹⁄₈in outside the embossed line. Punch a hole in the top of the tag.

▲ *A simple outline of evenly spaced dots makes a pretty decoration for small metal picture frames.*

3 Place the tag face down on thick cardboard and emboss a row of dots inside the marked line. Add other motifs as desired and glue on a photograph or message.

◄ *For extra charm add some small motifs such as stylized flower shapes or these simple stars.*

USING WIRE

Fine wire in silver, gold and other colours can be twisted into delicate coils and curls and used in conjunction with paper decorations, fabric or ribbon flowers, sequins or clay ornaments.

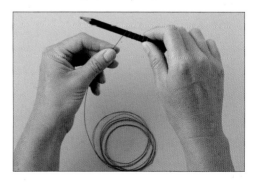

1 To make a coil, wrap some coloured wire around a pencil, then slide it off and trim.

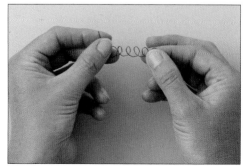

2 Flatten the coils with your fingers and glue the wire in place on the layout.

▲ *A wire coil makes an offbeat stem for a punched flower decoration in shiny plastic.*

INSERTING BRADS

Brads or paper fasteners are a decorative way to attach pictures.

1 To attach a picture to a tag, cut a small slit in each corner of the picture, and corresponding slits in the tag.

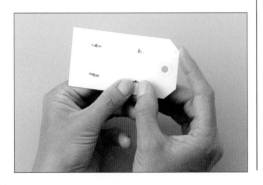

2 Push in the brads and open out the pins on the back, pressing them flat. Cover with small pieces of sticky tape if desired.

▲ *Brads can be used to hold layers of papers and embellishments together or they can be used for purely decorative purposes.*

▼ *This picture is held in place on its mount with eyelets in each corner, through which a length of fibre fringe has been threaded.*

INSERTING EYELETS

Eyelets can be used to hold several layers of paper or card together; in addition they provide holes through which ribbon or string can be laced.

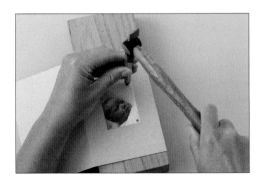

1 Glue the picture to the card, then place it on a block of wood. To make holes for the eyelets, place an eyelet punch in one corner of the picture and tap it sharply with a tack hammer. Repeat at each corner. Insert an eyelet into the first hole, through both picture and card.

2 Turn the card over. Place the pointed end of the eyelet setter into the collar of the eyelet, and tap it sharply with a tack hammer. This will split and flatten the collar. Repeat for the remaining eyelets.

▶ *Outsize coloured metal eyelets threaded with string make an eye-catching trimming for a plain frame.*

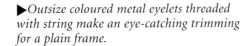

Adding texture and ornament

Relief effects add subtle interest to a page. Embossed motifs can underline a theme and draw attention to the tactile quality of lovely paper, while glitter and sequins add a change of texture as well as sparkle. Use tiny beads or model your own motifs for three-dimensional embellishments.

BLIND (DRY) EMBOSSING

If you are using good paper with an interesting texture, embossed motifs make the most of its quality and lend an extra dimension to a layout.

I Draw your chosen motif on a piece of card (stock). Using a craft knife and working on a cutting mat, cut out the motif to make a stencil for embossing.

2 Place the stencil on a lightbox, if you have one, and lay a sheet of watercolour paper on top. Use an embossing tool to press into the paper, through the stencil. This is now the back of your paper. Reposition the paper to repeat the embossed motif as many times as required.

▲ *It's possible to use real objects as templates for embossed designs. On very smooth paper you could try a finely detailed object such as a coin, while on heavily textured paper greater relief is needed. Here, a flat scallop shell has been used to embossed rough handmade paper with a bold design.*

◀ *Embossed on thick, soft watercolour paper this simple heart motif gains complexity when repeated and overlapped in a soft curve, creating an engaging interplay of light and shade.*

SHRINKING PLASTIC

I Using felt-tipped pens, draw a design on the rough side of a piece of shrink plastic. If the plastic does not have a rough side, sand it lightly first with fine glass paper. The image should be no larger than 12.5 x 10cm/5 x 4in. Bear in mind that it will become seven times smaller and the colours will intensify.

2 Cut out the image, leaving a narrow border all round. Bake the plastic in an oven for a few minutes following the manufacturer's instructions. It will twist and turn then become flat. Remove the image, which will be pliable, and place a weight such as a book on top for a few moments to keep it flat while it cools and sets.

GLITTER AND SEQUINS

If you want to add a little sparkle to a photograph, glitter paint is easy to control, allowing you to highlight fine details of the image. This product is particularly effective on black-and-white photographs.

1 Apply glitter paint to selected areas of a picture via the nozzle of the container or using a fine paintbrush.

2 Attach some small cabochon jewellery stones to the glitter paint, using a pair of tweezers to position them accurately.

3 Gently drop sequins and sequin dust on the glitter paint. Shake off the excess.

RAISED (WET) EMBOSSING

In wet embossing, a design is stamped on the paper then coated with embossing powder, which is fused with the stamped design using heat to produce a raised motif. Embossing powders and inks are available in many colours as well as metallic and pearlized finishes.

LOOSE GLITTER

Glitter needs to be attached to the paper using glue, usually painted on with a brush, so broad effects are easier to achieve than fine detail.

1 Press the stamp into the ink pad and stamp an image on to the paper where required. While the ink is still wet, sprinkle embossing powder over the image. Make sure it is completely covered, then pour the excess powder back into the pot.

2 Use a dry paintbrush to gently brush away any excess embossing powder from the paper.

3 Switch on a heat gun. Holding it about 10cm/4in from the surface of the paper, gently blow heat over the embossing powder until it melts and flows together to make a raised image.

1 Using an old paintbrush, draw the design in PVA (white) glue. Sprinkle on the glitter.

2 Shake off the excess glitter on to a sheet of scrap paper then pour it back into the container.

BEADS

Small glass beads can be strung on thread using a beading needle or threaded on to fine wire: 0.4mm is a suitable thickness to use.

◀ Mount a photograph on card using spray adhesive. Resting on a cutting mat, use an awl to pierce holes at each end where you wish to add wires. Thread coloured wire up through one hole, bending back the end on the underside to keep the wire in place. Thread on a few beads. Insert the wire through the next hole. Bend back the wire to hold it in place on the underside, and snip off the excess with wirecutters. Repeat to attach wires between all the holes.

▲ *In this celebratory layout, coils of fine wire frame the pictures in the central panel.*

BEADED FLOWER

Glass rocaille beads are available in a range of exciting colours and add sparkle and colour to layouts. When threaded on wire they can be manipulated easily to make motifs.

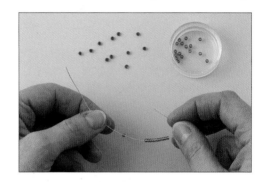

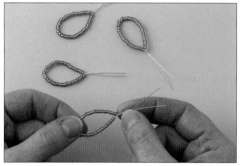

1 Bend back 3cm/1¼in of one end of a 12.5cm/5in length of fine wire to stop the beads slipping off. Thread on rocaille beads to a point 3cm/1¼in from the other end.

2 Twist the wire ends together under the beads to make a loop. Repeat to make four petals. Pierce the centre of a piece of card and poke the wire ends through the hole.

3 Stick the wire ends to the underside of the card with sticky tape. Splay the petals open on the front of the card and sew on a button to form the centre of the flower.

TASSELS

Little tassels made of silky thread are a charming trimming for elements such as small books containing journaling. They are quick and easy to make using embroidery thread (floss).

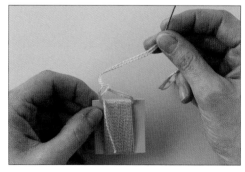

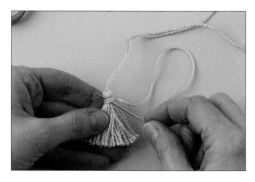

1 To make a tassel 4cm/1½in long, cut out a rectangle of card (card stock) measuring 8 x 4cm/3¼ x 1½in and fold it in half, parallel with the short edges. (Cut a larger rectangle of card to make a bigger tassel.) Bind thread around the card many times.

2 Fold a 40cm/16in length of thread in half and thread the ends through the eye of a large needle. Slip the needle behind the strands close to the fold then insert the needle through the loop of thread and pull tightly.

3 Slip the point of a scissor blade between the card layers and cut through the strands. Thread the needle with single thread and bind it tightly around the top of the tassel. Insert the needle into the tassel to lose the end of the thread. Trim the ends level.

Using modelling clay

Polymer and air-drying clays are ideal for moulding small three-dimensional motifs. Their fine texture enables you to create very detailed objects. Polymer clay needs to be baked in a domestic oven; air-drying clay hardens over about 24 hours. Glue motifs in place using strong epoxy glue.

CUTTING CLAY

For flat motifs, roll the clay out on a smooth cutting mat using a rolling pin. Rolling guides, such as two pieces of plywood placed on each side of the clay, guarantee an even thickness.

I Cut the clay with a craft knife. Cut straight edges against a metal ruler.

2 Use cookie cutters to stamp motifs then pull away the excess clay.

MAKING POLYMER CLAY MOTIFS

Complex motifs are easier to make if you first break the shapes down into a series of geometric forms, such as cylinders, cones, spheres and rectangles. These basic shapes can be pressed together and refined using modelling tools.

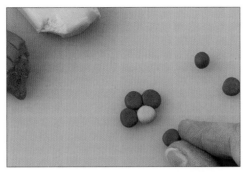

I To make a flower, roll a ball of polymer clay for the centre and six matching balls for the petals. Flatten all the balls and press the petals around the centre.

2 Shape the petals by impressing them close to the flower centre using the pointed handle of an artist's brush.

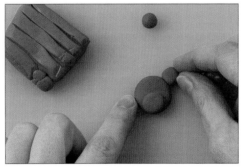

3 Roll a ball for a bear's head. and three smaller balls for the muzzle and ears. Flatten all the balls and press together. Impress the ears with the handle of an artist's brush.

4 Press on a tiny ball of black clay for the nose. Stamp the eyes with the glass head of a dressmaker's pin and use the point to indent a line down the muzzle.

STAMPING CLAY

For repeated motifs, flat shapes of polymer or air-drying clay can be stamped with any object with an interesting profile. Novelty buttons, for example, make good stamps. If the button has a shank, you can hold this to stamp the button into the clay. Bonsai wire (from specialist nurseries) is ideal for making wire stamping tools for curls and spirals as it is thick but very pliable.

◄ I To make a wire stamping tool, shape the wire using jewellery pliers. Bend the free end up at 90 degrees to form a handle.

▶ 2 Hold the handle and stamp the motif on to polymer or air-drying clay.

SEWING AND FABRICS

You can use fabrics and fibres of all kinds to add texture and variety to your album pages, and all can be enhanced with decorative stitching and embroidery, by hand or machine. Bold stitches also look good on paper and card (stock). If you are machine sewing on paper use a new needle.

STRAIGHT STITCH

Use plain machine stitching to join fabrics to paper or card (stock).

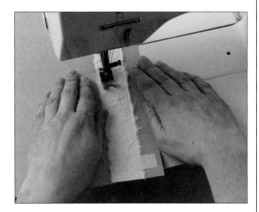

▲ For decorative effect or to apply a contrast coloured border, tear or cut a strip of paper or fabric. Tape it to the background with masking tape at the top and bottom. Stitch the strip with a straight stitch either in a straight line or meander in a wavy line. Remove the masking tape. Pull the thread ends to the wrong side and knot them. Cut off the excess thread.

ZIG-ZAG

In a contrasting colour, zig-zag stitch makes a decorative border.

▲ Stick a photograph in place with paper glue. Stitch along the edges of the photo with a zig-zag stitch, pivoting the stitching at the corners. Pull the thread ends to the wrong side and knot them. Cut off the excess thread.

SATIN STITCH

Decorative lines of satin stitch can be worked on paper, card or fabric.

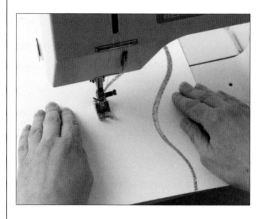

▲ To work a line of satin stitch on card (card stock) or fabric, gradually increase and decrease the width of the zig-zag stitch as you stitch. These lines are sewn with a shaded thread in random wavy lines. If you prefer, draw guidelines lightly with a pencil first. Pull the thread ends to the wrong side and knot them. Cut off the excess thread.

SATIN STITCH MOTIF

For a simple fabric motif, work the outline in satin stitch, using either matching or contrasting thread, then cut it out and attach with glue.

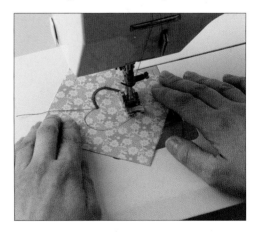

1 Draw the outline of the motif on fabric. Stitch along the line with a close zig-zag stitch, pivoting the stitching at any corners, until you return to the starting point. Pull the ends of the threads to the wrong side and knot them. Cut off the excess thread.

2 Use a pair of sharp embroidery scissors to cut away the fabric close to the stitching.

RUNNING STITCH

To keep your stitches perfectly even and avoid tearing paper or card (card stock), it's best to make the holes first using an awl.

1 Stick the photograph in place with paper glue. Resting on a cutting mat, pierce a row of holes along two opposite edges of the picture, using an awl or paper piercer.

2 Knot the end of a length of fine cord. Thread the cord in and out of the holes. Knot the cord on the last hole and cut off the excess. Repeat on the opposite edge.

GUIDE HOLES FOR HAND SEWING

Instead of piercing holes individually, try using your sewing machine, set to a long stitch length: the holes will be perfectly even and straight.

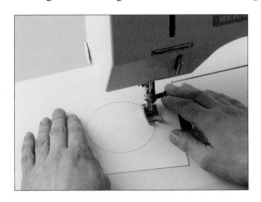

1 To create a frame or line of evenly spaced holes to sew through, first draw your design lightly with a pencil. Stitch with a straight stitch but no thread. Rub away the pencil marks with an eraser.

2 Sew in and out of the holes with thread. Knot the thread ends on the underside to start and finish. A photo or charm can be stuck within the frame.

CROSS STITCH

Use thick embroidery thread (floss) to make large-scale cross stitches.

1 Stick the photograph in position with spray adhesive and "sew" along the top and bottom edges with a row of large cross stitches using embroidery thread. To make it easier to sew, pierce a hole at each end of the cross with an awl, resting on a cutting mat. Knot the thread ends on the underside to start and finish.

▲ *A felt cover with a border of bold blanket stitching is a pretty treatment for a mini-album containing baby pictures.*

Working with fabric

A box of fabric scraps can be a real treasure trove when you are designing layouts. Materials such as net won't fray and looks lovely when gathered. Sheer organza is especially useful for subtle effects.

APPLIQUÉ

Bonding web is a fusible webbing used to apply fabric to fabric. It is simply ironed on, prevents fraying and is ideal for appliqué work.

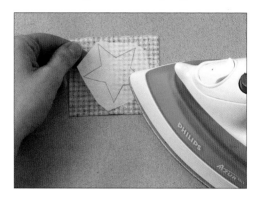

I Draw your motif, in reverse if not symmetrical, on the paper backing of the bonding web. Roughly cut out the shape and iron it on to the wrong side of the fabric.

2 Cut out the design. Peel off the backing paper and position the motif right side up on the background. Press with a hot iron to fuse it in place. Oversew the edges by hand or with a machine satin stitch if you wish.

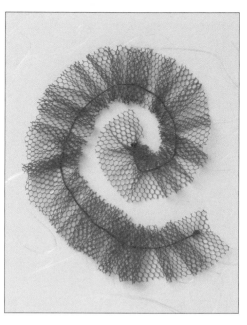

▲ *To make a pretty net spiral decoration, cut a 50 x 1.5cm/20 x ⅝in strip of net. Run a gathering thread along one long edge. Pull up the gathers until the strip is 15cm/6in long. Curl the strip and glue it in a spiral shape to your background using all-purpose household glue.*

ORGANZA LAYERS

This sheer fabric is available in many colours, some shot with silver or gold for exciting effects.

I Cut a motif such as this tree from fabric or paper and stick it to the background card (card stock) with spray adhesive.

2 Tear strips of organza fabric. Use spray adhesive to stick the strips across the card overlapping or singly in bands. Trim the organza level with the edges of the card. Glue on sequins to complete the picture.

▶ *Sheer fabrics such as organza can be layered to create depth and interesting tonal effects. Here the raw edges also suggest grass.*

TIE-DYEING

1 Wash and dry a piece of 100 per cent cotton fabric. Roughly gather the fabric in tight accordion folds and bind tightly with elastic bands where you want paler stripes in the design.

2 Dampen the fabric. Wearing protective gloves, plunge the fabric bundle into a bowl of cold water dye made up according to the manufacturer's instructions.

3 After the required soaking time, wash the fabric, rinse until the water runs clear, remove the bands and smooth it out to reveal the effect. Leave to dry then press with a hot iron.

NET SKIRT

A scrap of gathered net can be turned into a beautiful ballgown in no time.

▼ Cut a 14 × 6cm/5¹/₂ × 2¹/₂in rectangle of net. Gather one short edge tightly. Press a piece of iron-on interfacing to the wrong side of some matching fabric and cut out a bodice shape about 2.5cm/1in across. Glue the bodice and skirt to the background and attach a stick-on jewel at the waist.

RIBBON WEAVING

It's worth experimenting with ribbons of different widths to see what effects you can create. Once you're happy with the design, iron-on interfacing keeps it in place.

1 Cut a piece of iron-on interfacing to the finished size of your panel adding a 1cm/³/₈in margin at each edge. Matching the depth of the interfacing, cut enough lengths for the "warp" ribbons to fit along one edge. Lay them on the adhesive side of the interfacing and pin them in place along the top edge.

▶ **3** Press the ribbons with a hot iron to fuse them to the interfacing, removing the pins as you work. Press the raw edges under.

2 Cut enough lengths of contrasting "weft" ribbons to fit along one side edge. Weave the first ribbon in and out of the warp ribbons, passing it over one and under the next until you reach the opposite edge. Repeat to form a chequered pattern and pin all the ends in place.

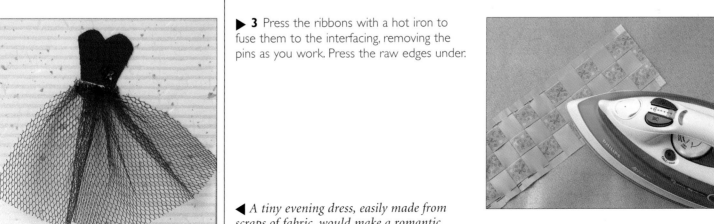

◀ *A tiny evening dress, easily made from scraps of fabric, would make a romantic detail for a party or prom layout.*

LETTERING SKILLS

While pictures are the focal points of scrapbook layouts, titles, captions and written details are crucial to creating lasting souvenirs that keep your memories intact. Word-processing software and the thousands of available fonts enable you to establish a host of different moods and characters for your pages, but writing by hand stamps them with a unique personality – yours. Perfect calligraphy isn't essential, but practising a few of the techniques that go towards mastering this traditional skill can be helpful in improving the grace and legibility of your own handwriting.

BASIC PENMANSHIP

A broad nib, pen or brush is the essential tool for calligraphy. When you hold the pen in your hand the flat tip forms an angle to the horizontal writing line (called the pen angle). It takes some adjustment to use this sort of tool after using pointed pens and pencils, so practising basic strokes is helpful.

Writing position

To produce beautiful work you need a relaxed posture, so spend some time adjusting your position so that you are comfortable. You may like to work on a drawing board resting on a table top, or secured to the edge of a table so that the paper is on gentle slope. If you prefer, you can rest the board on your lap, or flat on a table, resting your weight on your non-writing arm so that you have free movement with your pen.

Remember to place some extra sheets beneath the paper you are working on to act as padding: this will help the flexibility of the nib and stop it scratching the paper and spattering ink. Attach the writing sheets securely to the board with masking tape.

Light should fall evenly on your working area; although good daylight is best, you can also use an adjustable lamp to light the page.

Terminology

Calligraphy uses special terms to describe the constituent parts of letters and words and the way they are written. The style or "hand" in which the writing is created is composed of "letterforms". These are divided into capital, or "upper-case" letters and smaller "lower-case" letters. Most text is written in the latter because they are easier to read than solid blocks of capitals.

The "x-height" is the height of the full letter in capitals or the main body of

◄ *Calligraphy pens are available with different size nibs. This type of pen can be used with different colours and consistencies of ink.*

small letters, excluding "ascenders" and "descenders", which extend above or below the line of the text.

Calligraphers use pencil guidelines to ensure that their strokes are correctly placed on the page, and the two most important are those drawn to mark the top and bottom of the x-height.

Forming strokes

When you write with a normal pen, it can easily be moved round the page. When you are using a calligraphy pen this is not possible because the nib resists against the paper and may cause an ink blot or mark. For this reason, letters are made from several separate strokes, lifting the pen between them. For example, the letter "o" is made using two strokes, with one pen lift, while a small "d" is made in three strokes and other letters may require four. Practise slowly to start with.

WRITING WITH THE LEFT HAND

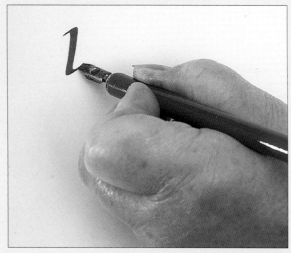

If you are left-handed you should sit to the right of the paper and tuck the left elbow into the waist, twisting the wrist so as to hold the pen at the required angle. Special left-oblique nibs are available to minimize the amount that the wrist needs to be bent, but if you can manage with straight-edged nibs the left-hander will have a greater choice of nibs available to them.

Three strokes

Four strokes

PRACTICE STROKES

To begin with it is helpful to practise just keeping the whole nib edge against the paper.

Practise simple curves and angles before you form any letters. Zig-zag patterns will show you the thinnest and thickest marks the nib is capable of.

PEN ANGLES

Holding the pen at the same angle to the writing line for every letter is an essential discipline to create letters that work well together. Practise first on spare paper. A line of differently angled letters will look odd.

Resist the temptation to move the wrist as you would in standard writing. As you complete each letter, check that you are keeping the same pen angle: it is easy to change without noticing. Zig-zag patterns, made at the correct angle for the alphabet you are using, can be a useful warming up exercise before writing.

LAYING OUT TEXT

Having decided what you are going to write, you need to plan where each word will fall and work out how much space it will take up, so that the page looks balanced and harmonious. Think about the relative importance of titles – and hence which will be larger or smaller.

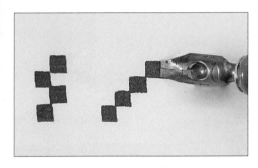

1 Determine the x-height of an alphabet using a "ladder" of nib widths. Holding the nib at 90 degrees to the baseline, make a clear mark, then move the pen up and repeat for the required number of widths.

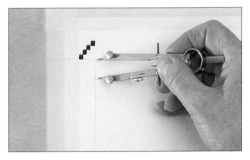

2 Measure the height of the ladder and use this measurement to mark the x-height down both sides of the paper, then join the marks up with a ruler and pencil. If you have a T-square you can mark one side only.

3 When ruling guidelines for lower-case letters, leave the equivalent of two x-heights between each line of text to allow for ascenders and descenders. For capitals, you can leave one x-height or even less.

4 When you are going to write mostly in lower case with the occasional capital, rule as for lower case and gauge the height of the capital letters by eye.

5 Once you start writing, it is important to be aware of letter spacing and awkward combinations, such as the "r" and "a" above: move them closer to create a natural space.

6 Adjusting letter spacing helps to make the text more legible by evening out the frequency of downstrokes: leave more space between adjacent uprights, as above.

Foundational hand

To grasp the principles of calligraphy it is best to start by learning an alphabet. The Foundational, or Round, hand was devised by the British calligrapher Edward Johnston (1872–1944), who is credited with reviving the art of penmanship and lettering in the modern age.

The Foundational hand is simply crafted, based on the circle made by two overlapping strokes of the pen, and is written with a constant pen angle of 30 degrees and few pen lifts. It is the constant angle that produces the characteristic thick and thin strokes of the letterforms. Johnston based his design for the lower-case letters on the Ramsey Psalter, a late tenth-century English manuscript now in the British Library. The capitals, however, are based on carved letterforms used in ancient Rome, and their elegant proportions relate to the geometry of a circle within a square.

The basic rules

Foundational hand is a formal, upright script, in which each letter is made up of two or more strokes. The letters should be evenly spaced for easy reading. An important characteristic of this hand is that the top curves of "c" and "r" are slightly flattened to help the eye travel along the line of writing.

The x-height is four nib-widths. Turn the pen sideways to make four adjacent squares with the nib, then rule your guidelines that distance apart. The ascenders and descenders should be less than three-quarters of the x-height (two or three nib-widths). The capital letters should be just two nib-widths above the x-height and do not look right if they are any higher. Hold the nib at a constant angle of 30 degrees for all letters except for diagonals, where the first stroke is made with a pen angle of 45 degrees.

Practice exercises

Almost all the letterforms of this hand relate to the circle and arches, so practise by drawing controlled crescent moon shapes, beginning and ending on a thin point. These semicircles can then be attached to upright stems to create rounded letterforms, or they can be extended into a downstroke to form arches. Begin high up and inside the stem to create a strong, rounded arch. Rounded serifs are used on entry and exit strokes to embellish the letters.

GROUPS

Round or circular

Note where the thin parts of the letters are. The first stroke of these letters should be a clean semicircular sweep, producing a shape like a crescent moon. Start at the top and move the pen downwards. The left and right edges of the pen form the circles.

Arched

The arch joins the stem high up. Beginning with the pen in the stem, draw outwards in a wide curve, following the "o" form. Start the letters with a strong, curved serif and end with a smaller curved serif. Keep the pen angle at 30 degrees throughout.

Diagonal

For the first stroke, hold the pen at the steeper angle of 45 degrees. This will prevent the stroke from being too thick. Take care not to make any curve on this stroke. Revert to a pen angle of 30 degrees for the second stroke.

Ungrouped

Keep the pen angle at 30 degrees for these letters. Follow the smooth shape of the "o" when drawing curves. Crossbars should sit just below the top line, and should protrude to nearly the width of the curve.

STROKES

(1st = red, 2nd= blue, 3rd = green)

▶ *The numerals and letters of the alphabet are written in a specific order. Follow the numbers on the digits and letters opposite to achieve the best effect.*

The letter "o" is made by two overlapping semicircular strokes, which produce the characteristic oval shape inside the letter. The back of the "e" does not quite follow the "o", but is flattened so it appears balanced. The top joins just above halfway.

For "a" draw an arch continuing into a straight stroke. The bowl begins halfway down the stem. The "u" follows the same line as an "n" but upside down, producing a strong arch with no thin hairlines. Add the stem last.

Start the ascender for "k" three nib-widths above the x-height. The second stroke is a continuous movement forming a right-angle. The pen angle is steepened for the first stroke of "v" and the second begins with a small serif. The two should sit upright.

The base of the first stroke of the "j" curves inwards to cup the preceeding letter "i". The second begins with a small serif and joins the base. The dot above the j is formed last. Start the "t" above the top line. The crossbar forms the second stroke, just below the top line.

1 A B C D E F G

2 H I J K L M N

3 O P Q R S T U

4 V W X Y Z & Æ

5 a b c d e f g

6 h i j k l m n

7 o p q r s t u

8 v w x y z &

9 ? æ ĕ ŭ é ß

0

DIGITAL SCRAPBOOKING

There is a whole range of software available for digital scrapping. Some of the programs that came free with your computer, printer or digital camera, such as simple layout software, or image-viewing and editing programs, are essential scrapbooking tools. Specific digital scrapbooking software is also available and is easy to use to import photographs and design elements to your pages. For those wishing to work at an advanced level, professional image-editing software enables you to create a vast range of effects on photographs and layouts.

SCRAPBOOKING SOFTWARE

If you enjoy scrapbooking and also like working on a computer, you will enjoy all the possibilities of creativity offered by designing your scrapbook pages on screen. Being able to undo, redo, or make several different versions of your ideas and see them side by side without wasting any paper, is a joy. Your computer and printer, with various software packages, give you all the basics you need to design and print great pages. If you also have a scanner, digital camera and access to the internet you will have even more creative options. There are many scrapbooking websites, which offer a variety of e-papers, borders and embellishments at high resolution, allowing you to make good-quality prints. They sell templates and even ready-made pages – so all you need to do is position your photos.

Each site has its own style: some elements look very high-tech and computer generated, whereas others have a more traditional feel. If you need inspiration you can browse through the galleries on the sites, which are full of exciting ideas. There are many software tutorials to help you out, too.

▼ *Scrapbooking websites such as scrapgirls.com offer themed collections of background designs, overlays, embellishments, and everything you need to compile your digital pages.*

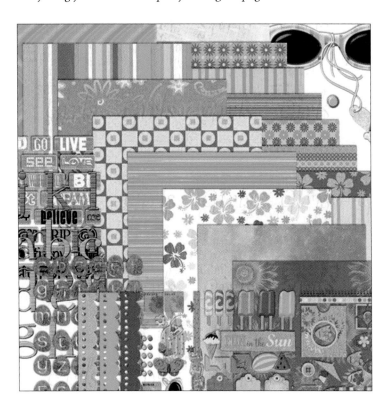

CREATING DIGITAL PAGES

Even the most basic software can be used to create backgrounds and make different shapes and frames to contain photographs and journaling. You can either use these in traditional scrapbook layouts by printing all the elements individually to arrange together on paper, or print the finished page. You can buy a whole range of papers to print on, and experiment with coloured and textured papers, and even fabric.

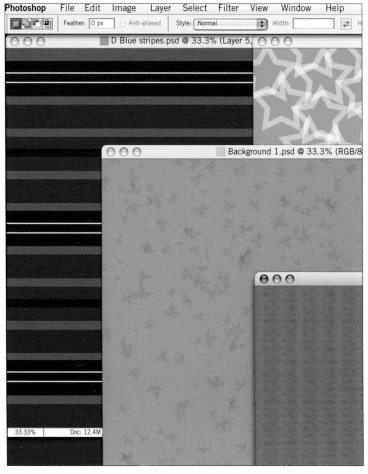

I To begin your page using image-editing software such as Photoshop, set the design area to 30 x 30cm/12 x 12in (it can later be reduced to 20 x 20cm/8 x 8in if you want to print on to A4 paper). For good printing quality use 300dpi (dots per inch) when creating and importing images, and experiment with different filters and effects. The stripes on the left were achieved by colouring rectangles then repeating down the page.

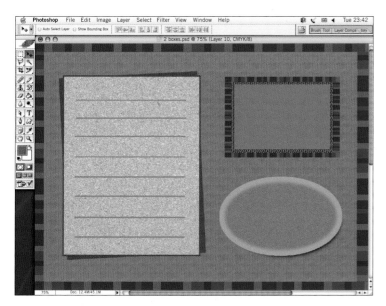

2 Squares, circles, stars and more can be created to make boxes, borders and embellishments, then coloured and treated with different filters and effects. Here the striped background has been used to create a stripy border. In the journaling panel on the left, a textured surface and rules imitate notepaper. The shape was duplicated then twisted a little and re-coloured to give a shadow effect. Another shadow under the oval shape gives it a three-dimensional feel. You can resize and reshape the elements as much as you like, until you are happy with the basic layout.

3 The beauty of creating journal boxes on screen is that you can type your story straight into the box, and then edit it and resize the type or the box until everything fits beautifully and you have exactly the look you want to achieve. Your computer will come with a basic range of fonts installed, and many more are available if you want to create a particular look. They can be enlarged, emboldened, italicized and capitalized and all will look different. Special effects for titles and other text include drop shadows, 3-D effects and outline lettering, and you can of course type in any colour to fit the mood of the layout. Alternatively, you can print the empty boxes and write the text by hand for a traditional look, or print your text on clear film and superimpose it on a printed background.

DRAWING A SOLID OBJECT

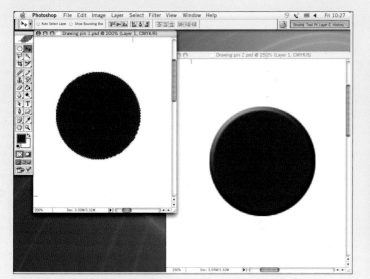

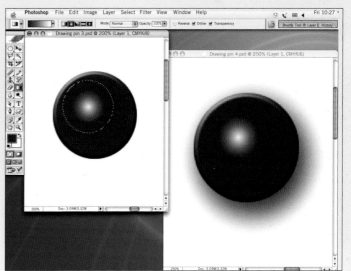

1 Try using imaging software to create the illusion of solid objects such as this drawing pin (thumb tack). Create a circle and colour it, using the eyedropper tool to pick a colour from one of your photos. Create a bevel edge using the Bevel and Emboss layer style. Here a smooth inner bevel has been added with a shading angle of 120 degrees. Play with the settings until you are happy with the effect.

2 To add a little shine to the surface of the pin, create a smaller circle on the surface. Choose Radial Gradient in the gradient tool menu and scale to make the area of shine as big or small as you want it. Here it has been set at 56 degrees. Finally add a shadow to relate the pin to the background, at the same angles of 120 degrees. You can now scale the image down to a realistic size and use it to "pin" your photograph to the page.

Scanning and using digital images

A scanner is definitely useful if you have an archive of traditional photographs you want to scrapbook digitally. All your old family photos can be scanned too, so all your relatives can have their own copies. As well as photographic prints, both colour and black and white, most scanners can also be used to copy transparencies and negatives. And of course your traditional paper scrapbook pages can be scanned, to be stored or refined digitally, or emailed to your friends.

Making a scan

1 Fit as many photos on to the scanner bed as possible, as they can be cropped individually once they are scanned. Work at 300dpi or, for small photos that you may want to use at, say, three times the original size, at 900dpi. Save and name the scan.

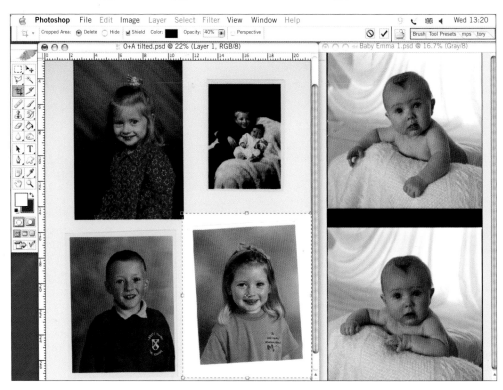

2 Crop out the picture you want to use, and save and rename it as a separate file. If the picture is a bit wonky, which often happens when scanning prints, or even upside down, it can be turned around easily in increments of 90 degrees or less, until it is straight. Check the alignments using the guides on the screen.

DIGITAL PHOTO FILES

If you have a digital camera, all your photographs can be downloaded straight to your computer using the software supplied with the camera. The pictures are then ready to use on digital scrapbook pages, or can be printed to use traditionally. Store each set of digital photos in a folder and label as you would ordinary prints.

You can store your photographs, and other scrapbooking material, on your computer, but they will take up a lot of memory. You should certainly delete any bad pictures so they do not take up valuable space, and it is best to copy all your pictures on to CDs or DVDs, so that you have back-up copies.

Use your camera for backgrounds such as beach, grass and sky, as well as other elements such as signs, tickets, labels and buttons. With these and elements from other sources you can build up a library of digital papers, embellishments and typography to use whenever you want.

NOW TRY THIS

1 Scan your photograph. Add a white border to imitate a print, by increasing the canvas size, before you bring it on to the album page. Duplicate the image box, twist by a few degrees, re-colour and put behind the photograph to give the semi-shadow effect.

2 Create stripes for the background, matching colours from the photo using the eyedropper tool.

3 Take a patch of colour from the photo background to use for the decorative boxes to the right of the photograph. Reshape one of these boxes to add the cross bands at the bottom and right of the page.

4 Create individual text boxes with shadows and add type to create the title.

5 You can make the drawing pins (thumb tacks) digitally as here, or print the page and then add buttons and other three-dimensional embellishments to the printed version. For best results use a good quality printing paper, and allow plenty of time for the inks to dry.

▲ *The denim dungarees Jack is wearing in the colour photograph provided the inspiration for this layout. The background is a picture of the garment itself, digitally augmented with stripes and lettering, and the photograph has been vignetted in a shape that fits neatly on to the pocket.*

▲ *A single scanned photograph of this pampered pet on his favourite cushion has been used three times at different scales, and the tartan rug in the picture also forms the background design. Don't forget that you can use a scanner to create digital images of fabrics and printed papers as well as photographs. The frames, name tag and stitching are all digital embellishments.*

USING A SCANNER FOR SPECIAL EFFECTS

As well as creating digital images from your photographic prints and negatives, you can use a scanner like a camera to create pictures of a whole host of other items that you might want to use on your scrapbook page. Different patterns and textures for backgrounds, traditional embellishments such as buttons, bows, lace, ribbon or photo corners can all be scanned to be used on your pages. All those tickets and other ephemera from your travels can be scanned in to go with the photos. In fact, if you can pick it up, then you can usually scan it! The flatter the item, the better the scan.

▲ *Woven fabric, denim from a pair of jeans, a piece of knitwear, flower petals and a child's painting have been scanned here. Fabric needs to be pulled taut across the scanner bed to avoid creases, unless of course you are after a creased effect. As with photographs, you can crop around the area that you want to use after making the scan. The scans can be used as they are, or layers, colours and other effects can be added to tone them down, creating more abstract patterns.*

1 Create a border around the knitwear background by duplicating the background, cutting out a row of stitching, copying this to the other side, then copying and rotating to make the other two sides of the square. Use the same method to make the edging around the photograph.

2 A felt flower with contrasting stitching is used here to embellish the frame. Having scanned the motif, use the lasso tool to cut it out and drag it on to your page. It can be resized as necessary and dropped into position. It can also be copied and used again and again in different sizes. Add a little shadow behind the motifs to enhance the realistic effect.

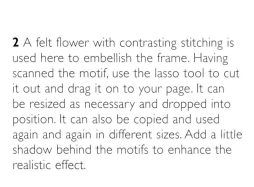

▲ *The final touch to this pretty layout is a row of simple felt shapes embroidered with the letters of the child's name. The pink knitted frame is a good match for this photograph, but you could of course change the colour if you wanted to use this texture in a different context.*

IMPROVING YOUR PHOTOS

Once you have your photos in digital format, there are a number of easy ways to enhance the quality of both black and white and colour photographs. Even the most basic picture-editing software packages will allow you to improve the colour or composition, or restore damaged prints. Always make a copy of the original scan to work on, so that you can refer back to it or start again if you don't like the new effect.

Cropping out distracting objects

If you find you have an awkward or distracting object in the background, or foreground, like this overhanging roof, it can often easily be cropped out using the crop or selection tool. Experiment with cropping even further to focus more on the subjects.

Improving colour

Here the picture on the left is too light and the contrast and colour have been improved using the automatic settings. To refine the result further you could alter the contrast and brightness controls manually, and add the colours individually in the colour balance panel.

Improving the sky

A featureless or dull sky is easily improved. First select the sky area using the wand or lasso tool. Select a suitable sky colour to go with the foreground, then select linear gradient in the gradient tool. Draw a vertical line with the mouse to add the gradient colour – the longer the line the more colour there will be in the background. Experiment with the gradient until you are happy with it.

Retouching

If you don't want to crop into the background of a picture, you may be able to remove a distracting object by retouching. Use the clone tool initially, to delete the object and match the area with the rest of the background. Then use the healing brush to soften any harsh edges. This method can be used to eliminate red eye, too.

Making a focal point

You can blur the background if it is too distracting and you want to focus attention on the subject. Use the lasso tool to draw around the subject and make a clipping path. Invert the path to make the background the working area. Now choose Radial Blur in the filter menu. Decide how much blur to apply and position the blur centre: in this case it has been moved down below the centre of the image so that the effect circulates around the subjects.

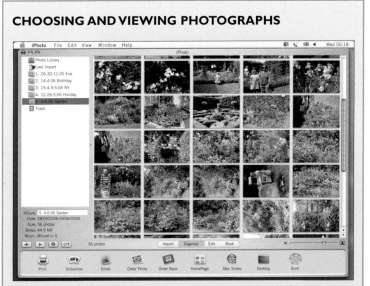

CHOOSING AND VIEWING PHOTOGRAPHS

Photo-viewing software is often supplied with your camera, printer or computer. It allows photographs to be imported from a digital camera and then viewed as large or small as needed. Viewing a group of photographs together as thumbnails makes it easier to make the best selection for a scrapbook page. You can arrange your picture library in folders or albums and add titles. Some software allows you to do a little picture editing too. You can rotate photos to view them the right way round, crop to improve framing and even create a slideshow. You can also import your finished digital pages to be viewed as a slideshow.

IMPROVING BLACK-AND-WHITE PHOTOGRAPHS

As with colour photographs, black-and-white pictures can easily be improved with the addition of special effects.

Brightening dark pictures

If a photograph is too dark, as on the left, make it brighter using the brightness control and lessen the contrast to lighten it. Use the curves and levels controls to refine the image. The sharpness can be improved too, which can be helpful with some older photos.

Repairing creases and tears

When old photos have been stored for a long time, they may be creased or damaged. They may also be stained and spotted with damp or mould. The clone tool and the healing brush are both easy to use to retouch any damaged areas, and tears, spots and even small holes can be repaired very effectively.

Creating tints and duotones

Copy the image (converting to greyscale if it is colour) then choose Duotone from the image menu. This allows you to create the photo in two, three or even four colours of your choice. Be careful – some colours, such as green, can make a photo look strange. Warm sepia works well with old photos. The duotones above show the effects created using orange (100y, 100m), yellow (100y) and finally magenta (100m).

Eliminating creased corners

Old photos often have creased or bent corners. If the damage is too bad to retouch in the digital version, you could try this effect. Draw an oval shape around the subject, then invert the selection so the background is selected and delete it. The edge of the photo is softened, or vignetted, by feathering, in this case by 30 pixels, before hitting delete. This gives a soft, period feel to the picture.

NOW TRY THIS

1 Scan a sheet of brown paper for the background. Add brush marks around the edges to create the effect of antique paper.

2 Add a white border to the photo, by increasing the canvas size before you bring it on to the page. Position it on the page, resizing to fit. Add a rectangular text box below and add the title.

3 Make a tag, or download a tag from a scrapbooking website. Position it at an angle in the corner of the page. Select a rectangular section of the tag. Copy this and enlarge it down the left side of the page. Tone down the colour by adding a semi-opaque layer over it.

4 Scan in photo corners, paper reinforcements and ribbon. Position the paper reinforcements, then add the ribbon as if threaded through them. Resize and crop to fit. Duplicate the ribbon and position it over the tag. Twist it around until it looks right and crop the length a bit. Add the photo corners. Finally, add a little shadow to all the elements to give a three-dimensional effect.

Dan & Joan

▲ The photograph of New York used as the background was given a painted effect using Fresco in the filter menu. In the main photo, Ink Outlines was used for the distant view, and Glass Distort noise effect has been added around the edge to soften it. A variety of city scenes have been added around the edges of the page to enhance the mood.

CREATING A PHOTOGRAPHIC BACKGROUND

Photographic backgrounds can be very effective provided they don't distract too much attention from the main subject. There are many ways to avoid this, such as keeping the background to a solid colour, reducing the opacity of the background image, throwing it out of focus or applying a filter.

1 Duplicate the background layer twice. On the top layer create a box around the area to be full strength, invert and crop out the background. You can check the crop by just viewing that layer. If you want to soften the edges, feather the crop.

2 Click on the layer below. Reduce the opacity, or strength, of the background in the layers menu until you get the effect you want: in this case the background has an opacity of 60 per cent.

3 To enhance the subject further, enlarge the full-strength area. Here this was subtly done by keeping the edge of the grass in line with the background. A soft shadow was added to lift it off the page.

CREATING A PANORAMA AND MONTAGE

Various programs are available to stitch panoramas together, but you can do this yourself. It works best if the pictures are taken from the same standpoint.

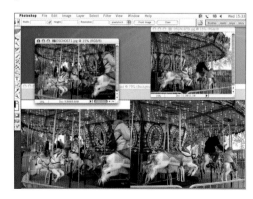

1 If you have an assortment of photos, choose the ones that match up best. Bring them on to the same page, resize as necessary and nudge along to find the best match. Enlarge the canvas to accommodate the photos.

2 To add people to the scene, cut them out using the lasso tool, and move them across to the panorama. They can be flipped, rotated and resized to fit. Use this method to add as many images as you need.

3 After adding all the images and adjusting them to fit into the scene, look at the edge of the final photo. If it is uneven it can be cropped, and the page area altered so that it fits a page or across two pages.

CREATING A TORN PAPER EFFECT

Torn paper is a good effect to master for use in your digital scrapbook pages. A real piece of paper can be torn and scanned, but it may not be quite the right shape. You can learn to alter the shape and size of a real paper scan or you can create a mock effect. Once you know how to create the effect with your software, this method can be used on any shape you need.

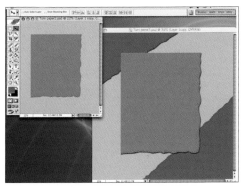
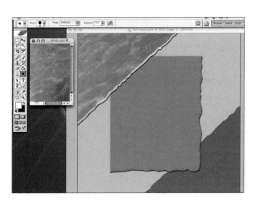

1 Create and colour a rectangle. Make a jagged line around two sides with the lasso tool. Join up the shape and hit delete.

2 Add noise in the filters menu and adjust the levels, making the torn area lighter or darker to suit your needs. This gives a jagged torn edge effect on two sides of the rectangular sheet.

3 This effect can be added to the edge of a photograph. Apply the torn paper method as described in steps 1 and 2, then use the dodge tool along the jagged edge so that it appears white like a tear in a real print.

CREATING A CALENDAR

Once you are into digital scrapbooking it is very easy to create your own calendar, adding seasonal effects. Scrapbooking websites offer many different calendar templates. Some can be created on the website and then downloaded to print (you will need broadband for this). Others are just like digital scrapbook templates and can be downloaded and designed as usual.

1 For this October page, create an autumn background from leaf-patterned paper with an opaque layer over it to soften the colour. Add numbered boxes, duplicating the required amount. Add the days of the week above each column.

2 Import the photos, resizing and moving them around until you are happy with the composition. Using the eyedropper to pick out a dark colour from one of the photos, add a border and shadows to both pictures.

3 Add a contrasting band at the top by creating a rectangular box and using the eyedropper to colour it. Add noise to create texture and place it behind the top of the upper photo. Duplicate the band and position one at the bottom of the page. Duplicate again and position the middle band across the foot of the lower photo.

4 Position the word "October" along the middle band, and add a shadow so that it stands out. Finally, using the leafy brush, spatter a few leaves in the bottom corner.

UPLOADING PAGES

Having made your digital page, you can save it to disc for posterity, and print as many copies as you like. The brilliant thing about digital pages is that you can also email them to friends, and even upload them on to one of the many websites that allow you to show them. If your pages are saved at 300dpi you should first reduce the resolution to 72dpi. This generally makes your page small enough to be emailed and uploaded on to the web. Follow the instructions given on the website for uploading your material for display.

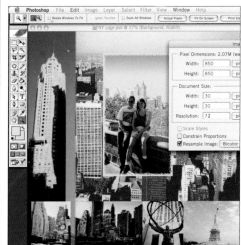

Styles to suit

For inspiration for the style of your scrapbook pages you need generally look no further than the photographs you want to display and your knowledge of their subjects. So while a collection of old family photographs, for instance, might seem to warrant a "traditional" treatment, your partying forebears enjoying their cocktails might look happier in chic Art Deco black and silver frames to echo their sharp suits and stylish dresses.

The fun is in relating your backgrounds and decorations to the contents of the pictures, and it's important that the photographs always have a starring role: the thousands of patterns and ornaments available from scrapbooking stores should never be allowed to overwhelm the personal elements of your displays.

Keeping it traditional

The photograph albums and scrapbooks of earlier generations have a wonderfully evocative look. It can be fun to adopt their style, either with squared-up presentations of photographs, or with a twist, by adding in memorabilia that has been digitally scanned or enhanced. Keep the presentation quite formal, with the pictures squarely mounted in narrow borders or in old-fashioned photo corners, and add handwritten captions.

▼ *This page, crowded with lots of tickets and other bits and pieces, evokes the eventful days of a memorable trip to San Francisco. It has been digitally created, and makes use of the standard elements of a traditional scrapbook.*

▶ *Athough created digitally, this layout looks back to an earlier era with its metal corners and hand-tinted black and white pictures.*

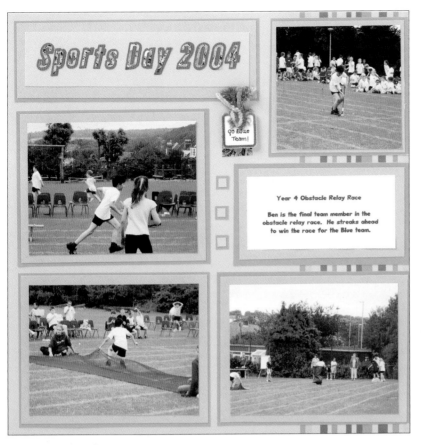

▲ The camouflage theme is taken from the uniforms in the picture and the titling and black border give a period feel.

▲ Here the pictures telling the story of the children's race almost fill the page, apart from a small panel describing what happened, and are squarely arranged with little embellishment.

▶ The dog's formal pose in this photograph has inspired an equally formal presentation in a double frame with bound corners.

▼ This record of a day at the zoo uses matching frames for all the pictures. The string detail is based on old album bindings.

▲ An old map has been used as the background to this Caribbean beach scene and neatly imitates the look of the sand where the boat sits in readiness to head out to sea.

Bold graphics

Crisp geometric shapes and repeating patterns can make really effective settings for strong images, or if you are using digital images, you could make a feature of the graphics within the photograph by repeating and blurring edges.

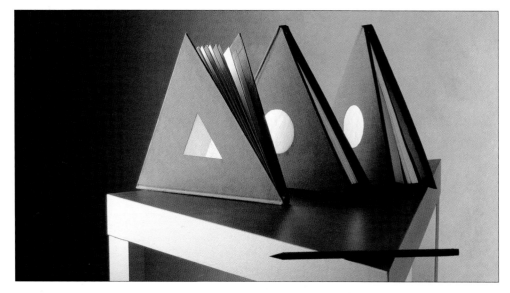

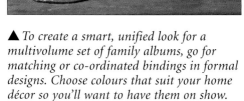

▲ *To create a smart, unified look for a multivolume set of family albums, go for matching or co-ordinated bindings in formal designs. Choose colours that suit your home décor so you'll want to have them on show.*

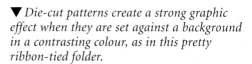

▲ *Albums need not be square: these striking triangular volumes have an Oriental feel and demand a modern, minimalist treatment on the pages inside.*

▶ *Papers printed in strong graphic designs like these make wonderful album covers. If you want to mix them up, look for designs of equal strength and scale, or use the same motifs in different sizes or colours.*

▼ *Die-cut patterns create a strong graphic effect when they are set against a background in a contrasting colour, as in this pretty ribbon-tied folder.*

▲ Although the carousel is a very traditional subject, the modern technique of digital splicing has resulted in an image that forces you to take a second look.

◄ Image-editing software has been used to add some eye-catching stripes to this digitally created scrapbook page.

▼ Royalty-free images from old black and white engravings can be photocopied and added to paper collages to make lovely album covers, cards and gift tags.

Fabric and stitch

If you are skilled with a needle, there are lots of creative ways to introduce textiles and stitching into your scrapbooking, from embroidered album covers to painted or printed silk panels or braided embellishments.

▼ *A small appliqué embroidery can become a front cover feature of a special album cover. This motif would be appropriate for a gardener.*

▶ *This small-scale book cover has been made by appliquéing small squares to a background fabric and blanket-stitching the raw edges.*

▲ Thick woven cotton or linen makes a lovely album cover, trimmed with embroidered titling and decorative blanket stitch and closed with two buttoned bands.

◄ For a contemporary decoration for the front of an album cover stitch small strips of evenly-spaced brightly coloured silk fabrics in a column to one side.

▶ Use transfer paper to copy a favourite photo on to fine fabric such as silk to form the centrepiece of an appliquéd panel.

Heritage

Most families have collections of photographs and ephemera handed down from previous generations, and it can be very rewarding to identify and mount them in albums to preserve them for the future. Good heritage layouts can be powerful evocations of the period when the pictures were taken.

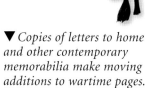

▼ *Copies of letters to home and other contemporary memorabilia make moving additions to wartime pages.*

▲ *Try to get older relatives to help you identify the subjects of photographs in your old family albums.*

◀ *Treasured souvenirs of long-ago trips deserve to be properly displayed and preserved for the future.*

▼ *A decorative collage in period style can make the most of simple but precious family snaps.*

▲ When you're assembling a family group like this, the photographs themselves may all be simple portraits, but with personal knowledge of the subjects of the pictures you can choose appropriate backgrounds that help to show what the people were really like.

▼ For old photographs that are to be out on display, use old materials in muted colours to frame them. Here an antique cream piece of card (stock) immediately frames the photograph, and the outer frame is made from coloured corrugated cardboard, which picks up the darkest tones in the photograph.

▲ If you've inherited old family albums they're likely to be crammed with small black and white or sepia prints. It can be effective to reflect some of that style in your new album, but it's often possible to improve the images greatly by scanning and enhancing faded prints and reprinting them on a larger scale.

Natural inspiration

Don't forget your scrapbook when you're out and about: as well as bringing home photographs, gather natural objects such as shells, leaves and flowers that will help you build up a complete picture of the places you visited.

▲ *This display box is a lovely way to bring together a photograph of a happy day on the beach with the collection of seashells you made while you were there.*

◄ *Instead of portraying a particular place, water has been chosen as the theme for this layout, bringing together diverse natural scenes. However, all the photographs used were taken in similar weather conditions, so the colours give the page a very unified feel.*

▼ *Handmade paper makes the perfect cover for an album on a natural theme. This sheet incorporates delicate scattered flower petals, and pressed flowers have been used to decorate the title panel. A simple undyed raffia tie holds it all together.*

▲ *This cover, decorated with a collage of leaves and flowers and bound with string, would be perfect for an album recording a garden tour.*

Cardigan Castle 2004

▲ *The complex frame-within-a-frame used in this layout, combined with the unusual view in the photograph, creates the effect of a window opening in the page, through which you can see the view of the tree beyond. The embellishment of leafy twigs is clearly related to the picture.*

St Agnes

▲ *As well as taking photographs of views and landscapes when you're on holiday, you can use your camera to record interesting abstract images and close-ups for fantastic borders and backgrounds in future scrapbooks.*

◀ *Pretty pressed flowers form the focal point on this handmade album cover. The cover is made from textured paper, which has a handmade quality to it. The flowers can be collected fresh in spring and summer and pressed at home.*

▼ *Trinket boxes are a delightful way to store small treasures that are unsuitable for your album pages because of their shape. Beautify plain boxes with patterned papers and embellishments such as pressed flowers and leaves.*

Simple colour schemes

A monochrome treatment is an obvious choice for a collection of black-and-white photographs, but it can also be extremely effective with pictures in which the colour range is fairly limited. Don't confine your ideas to black and white but explore other single colours that match or contrast well with your images.

▼ *A delicately decorated photograph box makes an elegant minimal presentation for a silver wedding souvenir.*

◄ *Although these striking seascapes are in colour the effect is almost monochromatic, and the simple black and white layout suits them perfectly.*

▼ *A crowded layout including photographs of all the members of a family is full of interest, and keeping it all in black and white gives a simple, graphic look.*

▲ *This all-white frame is intricately designed and texturally interesting, but doesn't distract attention from the photograph inside.*

▼ *Paper printed with a toile de Jouy design goes well with a strong collection of black-and-white photographs, though the plain black background is needed to keep all the images clear and well defined. The effect is softened with a purple border and ribbons.*

◀ *A fragile collection of old sepia prints can be overpowered by stark black-and-white or any strong colours, and looks best with gentle, faded tones.*

▲ *A photographic background, such as this drift of rose petals created for a wedding album, can have its opacity level reduced and be printed in just one or two colours, so that it does not compete visually with the photographs on the pages.*

◀ *In many older photograph albums the pages are of matt black paper, and this can still make a very effective and dramatic setting for both black and white and colour prints.*

▲ *A white wedding album luxuriously bound in white leather or vellum demands perfectly matted prints and a restrained approach to page layouts.*

Bold colours

When you are mounting photographs of happy children playing with brightly coloured toys or running about on a sunny beach, your backgrounds can be as bold and bright as possible to create an explosion of colour. You can either pick up one of the strong colours in the pictures and use a matching or contrasting tone for the whole setting, or go for a multicoloured effect, using all the colours of the rainbow for a really eye-catching layout.

▲ *The yellow background forming a frame around each of the cut-outs of this car has the effect of making them glow.*

◄ *Children's drawings and paintings, especially their self-portraits, make great additions to your layouts. Cut round both artwork and photographs to create amusing collages, and get them to help you with planning the pages.*

▼ *Here the layout is bold and bright but uses a limited colour palette and achieves a patterned quality by repeating two pictures all round the border. It also promises an irresistible surprise under the central flap.*

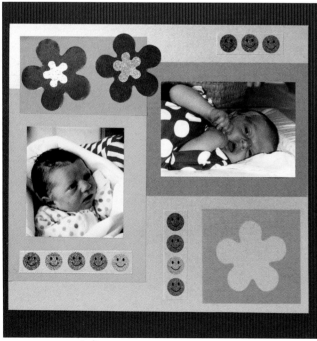

▲ *The two pictures on this layout are very different in character but the colour and black and white have been successfully linked by the shifting tones and consistent shapes of the frames and embellishments.*

▶ *Simple lacing through punched holes creates an eye-catching border for this name tag.*

▼ *This pretty garden of flower babies against a background the colour of a summer sky makes a sweet cover for a family album.*

▲ *This lovely page exhibits the finished results of the bold creative session that is in full swing in the photograph.*

◀ *The simplest shapes cut out of handmade or bark paper and cleverly combined make beautiful original tags and cards.*

▼ *Using a different bright colour for each page of a basic ring-bound album turns into it a really striking display that needs no further ornamentation.*

▲ *This digital scrapbook page takes the colour and movement of the sea as its theme, using a section of the photograph itself as part of the background.*

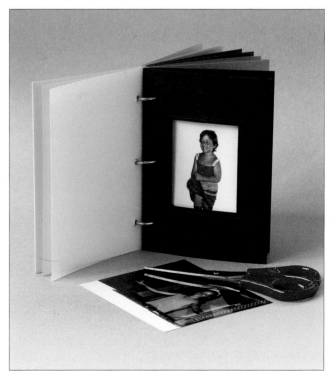

Pale and pastel

Delicately coloured photographs can easily be overwhelmed by a layout that includes strong or dark colours. Softer, paler tones mix and match well with each other and can be used to create a very feminine look, or to give a period setting for a collection of old and perhaps faded prints.

▼ *This pretty floral pattern looks right for the date of the photograph and its colours set off the sepia print perfectly. Toning stripes provide a crisp finishing touch.*

▶ *For a lovely, light-hearted wedding album cover, paste a scattering of tissue paper confetti shapes in mixed pastel colours over a sheet of soft handmade paper.*

Florence
Age 17

1940

◀ *Pale blue for a boy is enriched by the framing bands of deep blue and the toning pale shades of olive and brown in the background, which carefully echo the soft colours in the photograph.*

◀ *The ice blues of this layout emphasize the coldness of the snow in the photograph. Although the picture was taken in sunny weather there is no colour to warm it up.*

▲ *An enchanting little dog gets her own flowery setting in delicate colours that are just right for her light fur and small size. The daisy chain is threaded with a light touch across the bottom of the page. The simple colour scheme works well.*

▲ *Wearing a pale pink dress, this baby girl is given a traditionally coloured setting on a digitally created page. Touches of warmer pinks add interest to the treatment.*

▶ *The large spots on the girl's clothing were the starting point for this simple design, in which the colours are kept muted and pale so that the picture is the strongest element.*

Shabby chic

Mix-and-match patterns and textures with a confident hand for an eclectic, layered look with a timeless feel. This kind of treatment goes wonderfully with old family photographs and ornate memorabilia, evoking the richness of family history and the way in which possessions are gradually acquired and collected together in a home to make a harmonious whole.

▲ *Handmade papers in soft colours, which can often be found with flower petals or leaves incorporated in their surface, mix beautifully with pressed flowers, ribbons and other scraps to make albums and folders.*

◀ *Scrapbooking websites offer a host of different patterned papers, which can be used for onscreen layouts or downloaded and printed. Ornate historical patterns set off the elaborate dresses of past generations.*

▼ *There are plenty of gift wrap papers or poster-size prints available that can be cut to size and reused as attractive and decorative covers for an album. Choose a print that is appropriate for the contents.*

▲ *Colour-printed die-cut scraps were collected in the 19th century to fill scrapbooks and make decorative collages on items such as trays and screens. Reproductions are now available to add instant Victorian charm to cards and tags.*

▼ Richly patterned and gilded paper is ideal for embellishments such as envelopes and pouches to hold small treasures. Fasten their flaps with paper or silk flowers to complete the ornate effect.

▲ In the 19th century, the sending of greetings cards became extremely popular and many elaborate designs were produced, featuring flowers and hearts, intricate paper lace and ribbons. Their complexity and delicate charm provides inspiration for newly crafted displays in period style.

▲ The exuberant colours of mass-produced Victorian prints and scraps reflect the enthusiasm with which chromolithography, the first system of mass-market colour printing, was greeted when it appeared in the 1830s.

▲ A collage made up of old-fashioned items of ephemera immediately sets the tone for shabby chic. You could use this kind of background as a means of displaying old black-and-white photographs.

◄ Evoke the period of early photography with an abundance of intricate detail in scraps of lace and frills, printed patterns and rich textures. Delicate pressed flowers enhance the faded beauty of old textiles and photographs.

TEMPLATES

Copy and enlarge the templates illustrated to complete your scrapbook album pages.

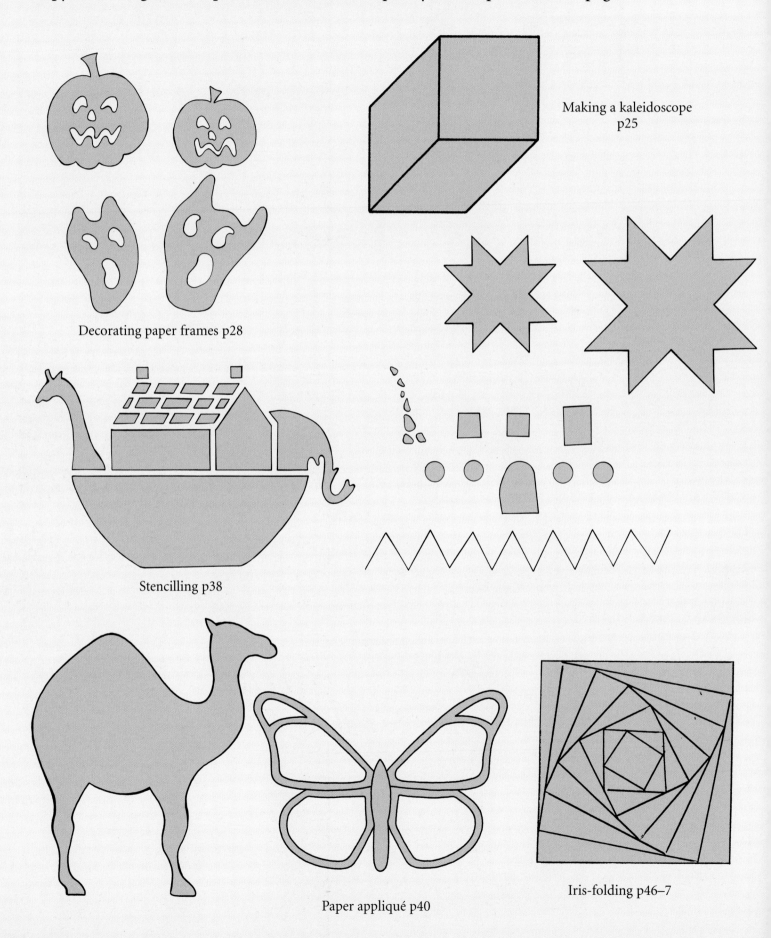

Making a kaleidoscope
p25

Decorating paper frames p28

Stencilling p38

Paper appliqué p40

Iris-folding p46–7

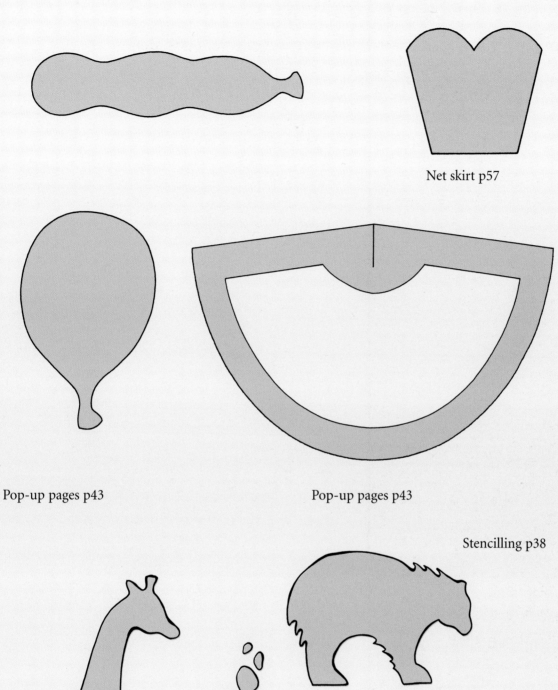

Net skirt p57

Pop-up pages p43

Pop-up pages p43

Stencilling p38

INDEX